THE ONE ACT PLAY

Its brevity is its greatest challenge and its greatest
strength. No other medium demands such speed of
movement, such subtle concentration of dialogue
and piercing insight into character. And none can
surpass its supreme moments of dramatic truth,
when in a single incident, an entire world and way
of life stand revealed.

In the one act play, young dramatists have found a
vital proving ground for experiments and innova-
tion. Within its bounds, established artists have
brought their distinctive genius into sharpest
focus. The ten plays chosen for this collection
represent the best in this tradition of excitement
and accomplishment.

TEN GREAT
ONE ACT PLAYS

Edited and with an Introduction

BY MORRIS SWEETKIND

TEN GREAT ONE ACT PLAYS

Bantam World Drama edition published May 1968
2nd printing....November 1970
Bantam edition published January 1972
4th printing
5th printing

Library of Congress Catalog Card Number: 68-19253

ACKNOWLEDGMENTS

The copyright notices are listed below and on the page following, which constitutes an extension of this copyright page.

SGANARELLE, *by Molière, translated by Morris Sweetkind. Translation printed by permission of Morris Sweetkind. All inquiries should be addressed to the Tranlator, c/o Bantam Books, Inc., 666 Fifth Avenue, New York, N.Y. 10019.*

THE BEAR, *by Anton Chekhov, translated by Alex Szogyi. Copyright © 1965 by Alex Szogyi. No part of this play may be reproduced in any form, by mimeograph or any other means, without permission in writing. Inquiries should be addressed to Warren Bayless, Creative Management, Inc., 355 Madison Avenue, New York, N.Y.*

HOW HE LIED TO HER HUSBAND, *by George Bernard Shaw, reprinted by permission of The Public Trustee and The Society of Authors, and courtesy of Dodd, Mead & Company. Originally published in 1913.*

SPREADING THE NEWS, *by Lady Gregory, reprinted by permission of Putnam and Co. Ltd. Originally published in 1904. The dramatization rights to this play are owned by Samuel French Ltd. of 26 Southampton Street, Strand, London, W.C.2, without whose permission in writing no performances of it may be made.*

To
David and Irene
Judith and Larry

Contents

The One Act Play

The one act play is a newcomer in the 2,500-year history of drama. It emerged as a separate artistic genre only in the last century. An important factor in its development was the establishment in several countries of anti-commercial theaters. In 1887 André Antoine founded the Théâtre Libre in Paris. Two years later a group of Germans established the Freie Bühne in Berlin with Otto Brahm as the first director. In 1891 the English dramatic critic Thomas Grein founded the Independent Theatre; and at the turn of the century the Irish Literary Theatre emerged in Dublin. Such theaters encouraged the production of naturalistic and symbolic one act plays in prose and verse.

In America the Provincetown Players, who organized in 1915 "to give American playwrights a chance to work out their ideas in freedom," produced many of the one act plays of Eugene O'Neill, Susan Glaspell, and Paul Green. In the first quarter of the twentieth century the popularity of vaudeville offered such dramatists as George Kelly, George S. Kaufman, and even Bernard Shaw the opportunity to write short plays, or "sketches." The rapid spread of the "little theater" movement in America encouraged the writing and production of one act plays. Today the staple fare of many off-Broadway theaters is the one act plays of Tennessee Williams, Eugene Ionesco, Edward Albee, and other contemporary dramatists.

What the short story is to prose fiction the one acter is to a full-length play, a related but separate genre with its own structure and technique. A good short story is not a condensed novel, nor is a one act play an abbreviated drama. By developing one episode, not a series of situations, a one act play creates a singleness of dramatic effect. Because of natural limitations of size, the one act play inevitably preserves the so-called "classical unities" of time, place, and action. Performed without a break, its unified tone can often produce a uniquely powerful emotional impact, as witnessed by the plays included in this anthology.

SGANARELLE

or

The Self-deceived Husband
(Sganarelle, ou le Cocu imaginaire)

by Molière

Prose Adaptation by Morris Sweetkind

ALTHOUGH *Sganarelle* is not one of Molière's mature masterpieces, it affords an excellent introduction to his plays. From the opening conflict between father and daughter, through the domestic battle between Sganarelle and his wife, to the quarrel between the youthful lovers, the plot moves rapidly from one amusing situation to another. Trifles which the deluded characters first accept as circumstantial evidence and then regard as conclusive proof trigger a violent explosion of emotions. Molière fully exploits the comic possibilities engendered by misunderstanding and self-delusion. Sganarelle later appears under various masks in other Molière plays as doctor, guardian, servant, and faggot-maker.

The perennial appeal of this comedy is attested to not only by its many performances in France but by its English imitators. In the seventeenth century, scenes and characters from it were adapted by Sir William D'Avenant, Thomas Otway, and Thomas Rawlins, and in the eighteenth century, by Charles Molloy, James Miller, and Arthur Murphy.

CHARACTERS

GORGIBUS (a middle-class citizen of Paris)
CÉLIE (his daughter)
LÉLIE (a young man in love with Célie)
GROS-RENÉ (his valet)
SGANARELLE (neighbor of Gorgibus)
WIFE of Sganarelle
VILLEBREQUIN (father of Valère, Célie's intended)
CÉLIE'S MAID
A RELATIVE of Sganarelle's wife

SCENE: *A Public Place in Paris.*

(*In front of the houses of* GORGIBUS *and* SGANARELLE. CÉLIE *in tears comes out of* GORGIBUS' *house, followed by her father and her* MAID.)

CÉLIE. Ah! My heart will never consent to that.

GORGIBUS. What are you muttering, you impertinent little girl? Do you think you can thwart my resolution? Haven't I absolute power over you? Shall the foolish arguments of your young brain override my paternal discretion? Who makes the law here, you or I? Tell me, who, in your opinion, knows what's best for you? Good God, don't provoke me too much or you'll soon learn whether my arm still has its old strength. Your best course, Miss Rebel, is to accept the husband intended for you. But you say, "I don't know his disposition and, if you will allow me, I ought to think about it beforehand." I know he is to inherit a large fortune. What else is there to worry about? Twenty thousand ducats possessed by a lover will more than compensate for any faults. Listen, I assure you with such a sum, he is a very worthy gentleman.

CÉLIE. Alas!

GORGIBUS. Alas? What's that supposed to mean? A fine "alas" she says! Listen, if you anger me any more, I'll give you plenty of opportunity to cry "alas"! I know the source of this nonsense. Because night and day you avidly read those cheap novels about love, you talk more about romantic heroines than about God. Toss those wicked books into the fire! Every day they corrupt the minds of youth. Instead of such rubbish you should read the elevating Quatrains of Pibrac,[1] the learned books of Coun-

---

[1] Guy Dufour de Pibrac (1528–1584), a distinguished diplomatist, magistrate, and orator who wrote popular moralistic verses.

cillor Matthieu,[2] whose work is full of fine sayings you can memorize, and another good book, *The Guide for Sinners*.[3] Such writings teach people in a short time how to live; and if you had read these books, you would respect my wishes.

CÉLIE. But, Father, how can I ever forget my undying love for Lélie? I should be wrong to marry against your wishes, but you yourself engaged me to him.

GORGIBUS. Even if you were engaged to him, the arrival of another man with a fortune annuls the engagement. Lélie is a nice chap, but remember that money is all-powerful, that gold makes ugliness charming, and that without it life is a sad business. I know you don't love Valère, but though you don't like him as a lover, you will as a husband. You can't imagine how the very name of husband endears a man to you, and love is often the fruit of marriage. Oh, what a fool I am to argue with you when I have the absolute power to command you. Enough of your impertinence. I don't want to hear any more of your foolish complaints. Your new fiancé Valère is coming here this evening. If you don't receive him graciously and kindly, I'll . . . Let's not discuss it any more. (*He leaves.*)

MAID. What, madam! You positively refuse what many other young girls ardently desire! You answer with tears a marriage proposal and delay your "yes," a word so agreeable to hear! Alas! if some one wanted to marry me, I wouldn't find it hard to say "yes." I'd say it a dozen times quickly. Your brother's tutor was quite right when in discussing worldly matters he said, "A woman is like ivy which grows luxuriantly when it clings to the tree but never thrives when separated from it." Nothing can be truer, my dear mistress, and I, miserable sinner, have found this to be so. May Heaven rest the soul of my poor Martin! When he was alive, my complexion was as rosy as a cherub's. My flesh was firm, my eyes sparkled brightly, and my soul was contented. And now I'm as depressed

---

[2] Pierre Matthieu (1563–1621), a French historian and poet who wrote didactic quatrains.

[3] A translation in French of a devotional book written by an ascetic Dominican friar, Lewis of Granada (died in 1588).

as an old godmother. In those happy days—which vanished as quickly as lightning—I went to bed in the depth of winter without kindling a fire; then even airing the sheets I considered ridiculous. But now, even in the dog-days, I shiver. Believe me, madam, there's nothing like having a husband in bed beside you at night, were it only to hear him say "God bless you" when you sneeze.

CÉLIE. How can you be so wicked as to advise me to betray Lélie and accept this unattractive suitor?

MAID. As far as I'm concerned, your Lélie is a fool for continuing his stay abroad. His long absence makes me suspect he's had a change of heart.

CÉLIE (*showing her in a locket a miniature portrait of* LÉLIE). Oh! Don't distress me with such sad forebodings! Art faithfully reflects his honest countenance and the steadfastness of his love.

MAID. It's true he does look faithful and honest, and you're right to love him tenderly.

CÉLIE. And yet I must ... (*She drops* LÉLIE's *picture.*) Help me ...

MAID. Madam, what's the matter ... ? Heavens? She's fainting! Help! Someone, anyone!

(SGANARELLE *enters.*)

SGANARELLE. What's the matter? I'm here.

MAID. My lady is dying.

SGANARELLE. What! Is that all? The way you screamed I thought the world was coming to an end. Let's take a look! Madam, are you dead? Um! She doesn't say a word.

MAID. I'll get someone to carry her in; please take care of her.

(SGANARELLE *holds* CÉLIE *with one hand and feels for her heart with the other.*)

SGANARELLE. She's cold all over, and I don't know what to say. Let's see if she's still breathing. Upon my word, I can't tell, but I do see some signs of life.

(*He puts his face close to* CÉLIE's *as his wife looks out the window of their house.*)

SGANARELLE'S WIFE. Ah! What do I see? My husband

holding in his arms . . . But I'll come down; he's certainly false to me, and I'll be glad to catch him.

SGANARELLE. She must be helped quickly; she'd be foolish to let herself die now. It's stupid to go to another world if you can stay in this one. (*He carries her in.*)

SGANARELLE'S WIFE (*comes out of the house*). He's gone and foiled my curiosity, but there's no doubt that he's unfaithful to me. The little I've seen proves it. I'm no longer surprised at his strange coldness in rejecting my modest love. The ungrateful wretch saves his caresses for younger women and starves me to feed their pleasures. These husbands are all alike: they become indifferent to what is lawful; in the early stages of marriage, they seem to be in love with us and are wonderful, but the wretches soon tire of our affections and carry elsewhere what is rightfully ours. Oh! How annoying that we can't change our husbands as we do our linen! That would be convenient; and believe me, I know it would please many neglected wives including myself. (*She picks up the locket which* CÉLIE *has dropped.*) But what's this? A jewel case I've been lucky enough to find? The enamel is beautiful and the workmanship charming. I'll look inside.

(SGANARELLE *returns, talking to himself.*)

SGANARELLE. They thought she was dead, but it was nothing at all! She's all right now. But here's my wife.

SGANARELLE'S WIFE (*thinking herself alone, she opens the locket*). Good heavens! It's a miniature, a fine picture of a handsome man.

SGANARELLE. What's she looking at so closely? (*He peers over her shoulder.*) Upon my soul, this picture bodes my honor little good. An ugly suspicion of jealousy disturbs me.

SGANARELLE'S WIFE (*not seeing her husband*). I never saw anything so beautiful in my life. The workmanship is even more valuable than the gold! Oh, how sweet it smells!

SGANARELLE (*aside*). Good God, she's kissing it! Now I understand . . .

SGANARELLE'S WIFE (*continues her monologue*). Oh, it

must be delightful to have such a handsome man for a sweetheart; such a temptation would be hard to resist. Alas! Why haven't I a husband like this instead of my boorish clodhopper?

SGANARELLE (*snatching the locket from her*). You hussy! I've caught you in the very act of slandering your dear, honorable husband. So, my worthy spouse, your husband is not good enough for you! In Beelzebub's name— and may the devil carry you away—what better match could you wish for? Can you find any fault in me? This shape, this manner that everyone admires, this love-inspiring face for which a thousand beautiful women sigh both night and day—in brief, my own delightful self doesn't satisfy you. To satisfy your ravenous desire, you want a husband only as an appetizer to the main dish, a gallant.

SGANARELLE'S WIFE. I get the drift of your abusive innuendos. You think by these tactics . . .

SGANARELLE. Please, stop making excuses. Here I have convincing proof of your misdeeds.

SGANARELLE'S WIFE. I'm angry enough. Don't provoke me by additional false accusations. Furthermore don't think you can keep my pretty locket. I'm considering . . .

SGANARELLE. Breaking your neck. I wish I had the man in my clutches instead of his portrait.

SGANARELLE'S WIFE. Why?

SGANARELLE (*sarcastically*). Never mind, dear. Sweet, faithful wife. I shouldn't complain. I thank you for the many favors received. (*He looks at the portrait of* LÉLIE.) So there he is, your darling, your pretty bedfellow, your secret flame, the gay blade with whom . . .

SGANARELLE'S WIFE. With whom . . . ? Go on.

SGANARELLE. With whom, I say . . . Oh! I'm bursting with vexation.

SGANARELLE'S WIFE. What does the drunken sot mean by all this?

SGANARELLE. Slut, you know but too well. I will no longer be called Sganarelle but Mr. Cuckold. Because of you I've lost my honor. The least I could do is to give you a good beating.

SGANARELLE'S WIFE. How dare you talk to me like this?

SGANARELLE. How dare you play me these devilish tricks?

SGANARELLE'S WIFE. What devilish tricks? Say what you mean.

SGANARELLE. Oh! What's the use of complaining? Truly, to wear a pair of antlers like a stag is a very pretty sight for people to stare at.

SGANARELLE'S WIFE. After grossly insulting me, you think you can escape my vengeance by stupidly pretending to be angry. I never heard of such insolence! The person who starts the quarrel is the real offender.

SGANARELLE. Oh! What impudence! To see her proud confident behavior, wouldn't you take her to be virtuous?

SGANARELLE'S WIFE. Go, flatter your mistresses, tell them you love them, caress them, but give me back my picture and stop jesting with me. (*She snatches the locket from him and runs away.*)

SGANARELLE. So you think you'll get away from me; but I'll get it back. (*He rushes after her.*)

(LÉLIE *and his valet,* GROS-RENÉ, *enter.*)

GROS-RENÉ. Well, here we are at last; but, sir, if I might be so bold, will you explain one little thing to me.

LÉLIE. And what's that?

GROS-RENÉ. Are you possessed by some devil or other that prevents your collapse from fatigue? For a whole week with whip and spur we've been urging on our confounded nags whose cursed trot has shaken every one of my limbs out of joint, not to mention the ache in an unmentionable part. Yet, here you are alert and hearty without rest or food.

LÉLIE. My haste can easily be explained. I'm worried about the report of Célie's marriage. You know I adore her. I want to find out if there is any truth in this ominous rumor.

GROS-RENÉ. Yes, but you need a good meal inside you to help clear up this affair. Your body and spirit would be strengthened to resist the blows of fate. I know from my own experiences when I'm hungry, the slightest set-back floors me. But when I've eaten a good meal, my strengthened spirit can resist anything, and the greatest misfortunes don't depress me. Believe me, stuff yourself well with unlimited quantities of food. The best protection against misfortune and sorrow is to fortify your heart with twenty glasses of wine.

LÉLIE. I can't eat a thing.

GROS-RENÉ (*aside*). I can eat very well indeed, so help me God! (*To* LÉLIE.) Your dinner will be ready presently.

LÉLIE. Shut up, I tell you.

GROS-RENÉ. What an impolite command!

LÉLIE. I'm upset, not hungry.

GROS-RENÉ. I'm upset and hungry to see this foolish love affair obsessing you.

LÉLIE. Let me get some information about my darling. Don't bother me. Go and eat if you like.

GROS-RENÉ (*bowing politely*). I always obey a master's orders. (*He hurries out.*)

LÉLIE. No, no, too many fears torment me. Yet I shouldn't despair, for her father has promised me Célie's hand, and she has given me proofs of her love.

(SGANARELLE *enters. He doesn't see* LÉLIE *and triumphantly waves the locket.*)

SGANARELLE. I got it back. Now I can leisurely inspect the mug of this rascal who betrayed me. I don't recognize him.

LÉLIE (*aside*). Heavens! What's this? If that's my picture, what am I to believe?

SGANARELLE (*not seeing* LÉLIE *and feeling sorry for himself*). Ah! Poor Sganarelle! What a sad fate to have your reputation sullied! I must . . . (*Perceiving that* LÉLIE *observes him,* SGANARELLE *moves away.*)

LÉLIE (*aside*). I have good reason to be nervous when I see this pledge of my love in other hands.

SGANARELLE (*aside*). From now on, I'll be the butt of jests. People will greet me by holding up two fingers; popular ballads will be sung about the dishonor that a wicked wife has stamped on my forehead.

LÉLIE (*aside*). Could I be mistaken?

SGANARELLE (*aside*). Oh! You tramp! The nerve of you to betray me in the prime of my life! You, the wife of a husband who is still considered handsome! Must a monkey-faced, damnable juvenile . . . ?

LÉLIE (*aside, still looking at the portrait in* SGANARELLE's *hand*). I'm not mistaken. It is my portrait.

SGANARELLE (*turning his back on* LÉLIE). This man seems very inquisitive.

LÉLIE (*aside*). I'm very much surprised.

SGANARELLE (*aside*). What does he want?

LÉLIE (*aside*). I'll speak to him. (*Aloud.*) May I . . . have a word with you?

(SGANARELLE *backs away from him.*)

SGANARELLE (*aside, moving still farther away*). What does he want to tell me now?

LÉLIE. I'm curious to know how you got hold of that picture.

SGANARELLE (*looks at* LÉLIE *and examines the picture more closely. Aside*). Why does he want to know? But, come to think of it . . . Upon my word, now I know what's upset him. I'm no longer surprised. This is my man, or rather, my wife's man.

LÉLIE. Please relieve my anxiety and tell me where you obtained . . .

SGANARELLE. Thank you, I know what disturbs you. This lifelike portrait, the cause of your anxiety, belonged to a certain female acquaintance of yours. The amorous intrigues conducted by that lady and you are no secret to me. I don't know if I have the honor of being known by your gallant lordship, but from now on, be kind enough to terminate this immoral relationship which violates the holy bonds of matrimony, for . . .

LÉLIE. What's this you say? She from whom you received this pledge . . . ?

SGANARELLE. Is my wife, and I am her husband.

LÉLIE. Her husband?

SGANARELLE. Yes, her husband, I assure you; married but not merry. And you know the reason. I'm going to tell her family about the affair without delay. (*He leaves.*)

LÉLIE. Good God! What have I heard! The report that her husband was the ugliest man then was true. Even if your faithless lips had never sworn eternal love more than a thousand times, the disgust you should have felt at such a shameful choice would have been enough to preserve our love . . . But this outrage to my pride and the exhaustion of a long journey have so upset me that I feel weak and shaky.

(SGANARELLE'S WIFE *enters.*)

SGANARELLE'S WIFE. In spite of me, my treacherous . . . (*Seeing* LÉLIE.) What's the trouble? You look, sir, as if you're about to collapse.

LÉLIE. It must have been a sudden shock.

SGANARELLE'S WIFE. I'm afraid you're going to faint. Come in the house and rest until you feel better.

LÉLIE. You're very kind. I'll just stay for a few minutes.

(*They go inside.* SGANARELLE *and the* RELATIVE *of his wife appear.*)

RELATIVE. I sympathize with a husband's anxiety in a case like this, but aren't you a little too hasty in taking offense? What you've told me about her, kinsman, is not conclusive proof of her guilt. It's a delicate subject, and one shouldn't be accused of such a crime unless it can be fully proved.

SGANARELLE. You mean I have to catch her in the act?

RELATIVE. Rashness leads us to make mistakes. Who knows how she got this picture and, after all, whether she even knows this man. Investigate the matter further; and if your suspicion is confirmed, I'll be the first to punish her offense. (*He leaves.*)

SGANARELLE. That's good advice. The best way really is to proceed cautiously. Perhaps my excited imagination is deceiving me, and the sweat on my brow is premature. The picture which threw such a scare into me doesn't positively confirm my dishonor. Watching my step . . .

(SGANARELLE'S WIFE *shows* LÉLIE *out of her house.*)

SGANARELLE (*aside, seeing them*). What's this? Death and damnation! The picture doesn't matter any more. Here in the flesh is the original.

SGANARELLE'S WIFE (*to* LÉLIE). Your stay was much too brief. If you leave too soon, you may have a relapse.

LÉLIE. No, no. I'm most grateful to you for your kind assistance.

SGANARELLE (*aside*). He covers up his shamelessness with gallantry!

(*She goes into house.*)

He's noticed me. Let's hear what he's going to say.

LÉLIE (*aside*). Oh! I'm terribly disturbed and that ugly husband is responsible . . . but I must master this futile hatred and attribute my sufferings to the harshness of fate. Yet I can't keep envying his good fortune in love. (*To* SGANARELLE.) You're a lucky man to have such a beautiful wife.

(CÉLIE *appears just as* LÉLIE *leaves.* SGANARELLE *does not see her.*)

SGANARELLE. Well, that was clear as daylight. His extraordinary remarks make me feel as if horns were sprouting out of my head. (*Calling out to the departed* LÉLIE.) Listen here, you haven't acted like an honorable man.

CÉLIE (*aside*). Wasn't that Lélie I just saw? Why didn't he tell me he'd returned?

SGANARELLE (*without seeing* CÉLIE). "You're a lucky man to have such a beautiful wife." Say rather an unlucky man whose disgraceful wife has undoubtedly deceived him.

(CÉLIE *slowly approaches but waits for him to finish his tantrum.*)

Yet I let him get away, and I stand here with my arms folded like a foolish blockhead. I should at least have knocked his hat off, flung stones at him, or muddied his cloak. To appease my wrath I ought to rouse the whole neighborhood and shout, "Stop that dishonorable thief!"

CÉLIE (*to* SGANARELLE). Pardon me, do you happen to know the gentleman who spoke to you and just left?

SGANARELLE. Alas! My wife's the one who knows him, madam, not I.

CÉLIE. What's upset you?

SGANARELLE. Don't blame me for this unseasonable sorrow. My abundant sighs are simply an expression of my suffering.

CÉLIE. What's the cause of this profound grief?

SGANARELLE. I'm not distressed because of some trifle. I challenge anyone not to grieve if he found himself in my situation. In me you see the perfect model of an unhappy husband. Poor Sganarelle has not only been stripped of his honor but deprived of his reputation as well.

CÉLIE. How?

SGANARELLE. That foppish philanderer—begging your pardon, madam—has made me a cuckold. Why, this very day I witnessed a secret meeting between him and my wife.

CÉLIE. You mean the man who now . . .

SGANARELLE. Yes, yes, he disgraced me. He's in love with my wife and she with him.

CÉLIE. I had a presentiment his secret return covered up some base design. I trembled the moment I saw him withdraw.

SGANARELLE. You're very kind to come to my support; not everybody is so charitably distressed. Some who have heard of my martyrdom instead of taking my part have only laughed at me.

CÉLIE. What punishment is appropriate for such a vile deed? Is such a polluted person fit to live? Heavens! How could it happen?

SGANARELLE. It did to me.

CÉLIE. O traitor! Villain! Deceitful, faithless scoundrel!

SGANARELLE. What a darling creature!

CÉLIE. No, no, there aren't enough tortures in hell to punish him for his crime!

SGANARELLE. That's what I like to hear!

CÉLIE. Abusing both innocence and goodness!

SGANARELLE (*sighing aloud*). Ah, yes!

CÉLIE. To heap insult and contempt on such an unde-
serving heart!

SGANARELLE. That's true.

CÉLIE. A man who far from . . . but I'll say no more
or my heart will burst with grief.

SGANARELLE. There, there, dear lady, don't be so upset.
I'm deeply touched by this expression of grief at my misfortune.

CÉLIE. Don't think that I'm just going to sit down and
lament. No, my heart knows what to do to be avenged.
Nothing will stop me. (*She leaves.*)

SGANARELLE. May heaven protect her from every danger! How kind of her to wish to avenge me! After such
a noble display of wrath inspired by my disgrace, I must
act. Only a cowardly fool would endure such insults. I'll
find this rascal who has disgraced me and prove my courage by avenging my dishonor. I'll teach you, you scoundrel, to laugh at my expense and to go around seducing
wives. (*He strides forward resolutely, but after three or
four steps, comes back again.*) Take it easy! This fellow
looks as if he were hotheaded and passionate. Heaping insult upon insult he may give me a beating, fore and aft.
I detest hot-tempered people; I prefer peaceful ones. I'm
not belligerent, for I'm afraid of getting a licking. My
outstanding virtue is a gentle disposition. Yet my honor
tells me that such an outrage must be avenged. Let honor
say what it likes, the deuce take him who listens. Suppose I play the hero and am rewarded by getting a sharp
sword thrust into my belly; and when the news of my
death spreads through the town, my honor, how much
will you be worth then? The grave is a very melancholy
and unhealthy place for those who are afraid of the colic.
As far as I'm concerned after careful consideration, I prefer to be a cuckold rather than a corpse. What's the harm
in it? After all, does it cripple a man's leg? Does it spoil
his shape? The devil take the inventor of the delusion of
grievance, linking the honor of the wisest man to the fickle-
ness of a woman. Since a person can be responsible only
for his own crimes, how can our honor, in this case, be

considered criminal? We're being blamed for the misdeeds
of others. If our wives have an affair without our knowledge, we have to suffer the consequences. They commit
the crime and we're declared guilty! The law should do
something about correcting such a villainous injustice.
Aren't there enough inevitable misfortunes in our lives?
As if our lives were not sufficiently troubled by quar-
rels, lawsuits, hunger, thirst, and sickness, we fill our
stupid heads with grievances which have no reality. Let
us despise such idle fears and banish sighs and tears. If
my wife has done some wrong, let *her* cry; why should
innocent I weep? That I'm not the only one in this fix
is some consolation. Many people of rank see their wives
seduced and don't say a word about it. Why should I
then pick a quarrel for a trifling insult? They'll call me
a fool for not getting revenge, but I'd be a greater fool
to get myself killed. (*Putting his hand on his abdomen.*)
Still, feeling the bile circulating here, I am almost per-
suaded to perform some manly deed. Yes, anger gets the
better of me; I can't really be such a coward! I'll get
revenge on that crook. As a start while I'm in this inflam-
matory mood, I'm going to tell everybody he's seduced
my wife. (*He goes out.*)

(GORGIBUS *enters with* CÉLIE *and her* MAID.)

CÉLIE. Yes, Father, I'll submit to your wishes. You're
free to dispose of my heart and hand. I'll sign the marriage
contract whenever you please, for I'm now determined to
do my duty. Having control of my former feelings I'll
carry out your orders.

GORGIBUS. That's what I like to hear. Upon my word,
I'm so delighted that I'd dance a jig if people wouldn't
laugh at me. Come here, my child, and let me kiss you.
There's no harm in that. A father may kiss his daughter
without creating a scandal. Your good upbringing as evident in your obedience has made me so happy, I feel ten
years younger. (*He goes out cheerfully.*)

MAID. I'm surprised at this change in you.

CÉLIE. When you know my reasons, you'll agree with
me.

MAID. Perhaps I will.

CÉLIE. That treacherous Lélie has broken my heart. He's come back without . . .

MAID. But here he comes.

(LÉLIE *enters*.)

LÉLIE. Before we part forever, I want at least to tell you . . .

CÉLIE. How dare you speak to me again! Such audacity!

LÉLIE. The audacity may be great, but if I didn't reproach you for your choice, I'd feel guilty. Live, live happily, respect your husband's love and forget me.

CÉLIE. Yes, traitor, I'll live so and hope earnestly that my happiness will bring you nothing but unhappiness.

LÉLIE. Why are you so angry with me?

CÉLIE. Why do you pretend such innocent surprise?

(SGANARELLE *enters, armed to the teeth*.)

SGANARELLE. War, deadly war I'll wage against this dishonorable thief who's put a blot on my escutcheon.

CÉLIE (*to* LÉLIE, *pointing to* SGANARELLE). Look at that man and you'll get your answer.

LÉLIE. Oh! I see . . .

CÉLIE. Isn't a glimpse of him enough to abash you?

LÉLIE. You're the one that ought to blush.

SGANARELLE. My wrath is rising by the minute. Mounted on its mighty steeds, my courage is ready to attack and blood will be shed. Yes, I've vowed to kill him and nothing will hold me back. When I find him, I'll dispatch him quickly to hell. I'll stab him right through the middle of his heart. (*He lunges with his sword and dagger*.)

LÉLIE (*turning around*). Stab whom?

SGANARELLE. Whom? Nobody.

LÉLIE. Then why all these weapons?

SGANARELLE. These? Just a protection from the rain. (*Aside.*) What a satisfaction it would be to kill him! Pluck up courage and do it.

LÉLIE. What?

SGANARELLE. I didn't say anything. (*He punches him-*

self in the stomach and slaps his face to raise his courage. Aside.) Chickenhearted coward!

CÉLIE. That ought to satisfy you, but you still seem offended.

LÉLIE. Yes, I am. Now I know you're guilty of the most outrageous infidelity and you've made a mockery of faithful love.

SGANARELLE (*aside*). Oh, if I only had an ounce of courage!

CÉLIE (*to* LÉLIE). That's enough, you traitor. I won't listen to any more of your insolent cruelty.

SGANARELLE (*aside*). You see, Sganarelle, she's on your side. Courage, my boy, take the offensive. Be bold and stab him in the back.

LÉLIE (*moving accidentally a few steps back, he meets* SGANARELLE *who was drawing near to kill him*). Since my words only kindle your wrath, madam, I'm satisfied, if you are, and I congratulate you on the lovely choice you've made.

CÉLIE. Yes, yes, I'm delighted with it.

LÉLIE. Go ahead, what else can you do but defend it?

SGANARELLE. Of course, she should defend it, but your actions, sir, are violations of the law. I have cause for complaint; and if I weren't a prudent gentleman, plenty of blood would be shed.

LÉLIE. What are you complaining about? And why this surly . . .

SGANARELLE. Don't say another word. You know who's the goat here. But your conscience and the danger to your immortal soul should remind you that my wife is my wife, and to make her yours under my very nose is not the act of a good Christian.

LÉLIE. What a base and ridiculous suspicion! You don't have to worry about that: I know she belongs to you and far from being in love with . . .

CÉLIE. Oh! Traitor! You certainly know how to lie!

LÉLIE. What! Do you imagine I could entertain one thought that would offend this man? Would you accuse me of such a cowardly act?

CÉLIE. Ask him, ask him! He'll give you all the facts.

SGANARELLE (*to* CÉLIE). No, you can argue much better than I can. Perhaps you can straighten out the affair.

(SGANARELLE'S WIFE *and* CÉLIE'S MAID *enter.*)

SGANARELLE'S WIFE (*angrily to* CÉLIE). I'm not the type to fly into a jealous rage, madam, but I'm not a blind fool. Some strange love affairs are going on here. You should make better use of your charms than to seduce a heart which rightfully belongs to me.

CÉLIE. What a simple-minded statement!

SGANARELLE (*to his wife*). Impudent slut, who asked you to butt in? She comes to my defense and you scold her. You're only frightened you'll lose your lover.

CÉLIE. Madam, I don't envy you. (*Turning to* LÉLIE.) Now that you see it's a lie, I'm delighted.

LÉLIE. What does all this mean?

CÉLIE'S MAID. Upon my word, isn't it time this mess was cleared up? For some time I've tried to grasp what's going on, but the more I hear, the less I understand. Really I think I ought to interfere. (*Placing herself between* LÉLIE *and* CÉLIE.) Answer me one at a time. (*To* LÉLIE.) What do you accuse this lady of?

LÉLIE. Of infidelity. She forsook me for another. As soon as I heard she was going to be married, I rushed back driven by an irresistible love, certain that she'd never forget me. When I arrived, I found her married.

MAID. Married? To whom?

LÉLIE (*pointing to* SGANARELLE). To him.

MAID. What? To him!

LÉLIE. Yes, to him.

MAID. Who told you that?

LÉLIE. He did today.

MAID (*to* SGANARELLE). Is this true?

SGANARELLE. I? I only said I was the husband of my wife.

LÉLIE. Just now when you looked at my picture, you seemed deeply moved.

SGANARELLE. Yes, here it is.

LÉLIE. You also told me that she who gave you this token of her love was your wife.

SGANARELLE. That's right. (*Pointing to his wife.*) If I hadn't snatched it from her, I wouldn't have discovered her wickedness.

SGANARELLE'S WIFE. What do you mean by your groundless complaint? I found this picture by accident in the street. After you had stormed at me in a jealous rage, I saw this gentleman (*Pointing to* LÉLIE.) nearly fainting and made him go indoors to rest. But I didn't identify him with the portrait.

CÉLIE. I'm responsible for the loss of the locket; I dropped it when I fainted and then you (*Pointing to* SGA-NARELLE.) kindly carried me into the house.

MAID. You see, if it weren't for my common-sense intervention, you'd still be victims of this crazy confusion.

SGANARELLE. Did all this really happen to us? It certainly threw a scare into me.

SGANARELLE'S WIFE. I haven't yet recovered from my fright. Although I don't like to be deceived, I'm not sure all my suspicions were false.

SGANARELLE (*to his wife*). Well, we consider ourselves honorable people. Since I risk more than you, why not accept my proposal to make up.

SGANARELLE'S WIFE. Agreed, but if I discover anything, God help you!

CÉLIE (*to* LÉLIE *after whispering together*). Good heavens, if this is true, what have I done? It's all my fault and I'll have to suffer the consequences. Thinking you false and wanting revenge, I unfortunately gave in to my father's wishes and became engaged to a man whom I'd always rejected. I made a promise to my father and what grieves me most is . . . But here he comes.

(GORGIBUS *enters.*)

LÉLIE. Sir, you see I've returned, deeply in love, and now I expect you to keep your promise, which gave me hope to marry Célie, and so reward my ardent love.

GORGIBUS (*sarcastically*). Sir, I see you've returned, deeply in love, and now you expect me to keep my promise, which gave you hope to marry Célie, and so reward your ardent love. I remain your lordship's most humble and obedient servant; my answer is "No."

LÉLIE. Is this, sir, the way you keep your promise?

GORGIBUS. Yes, sir, that's the way I see my duty and my daughter will obey me too.

CÉLIE. My duty, Father, compels me to urge you to honor your promise to Lélie.

GORGIBUS. Is this the way a daughter should obey her father? You're certainly fickle in your affections toward Valère . . . But here comes his father to make the final arrangements for the wedding.

(VILLEBREQUIN *enters*.)

What brings you here, Mr. Villebrequin?

VILLEBREQUIN. An important secret that I learned this morning cancels our agreement. My son, whom your daughter was going to wed, has deceived everybody. He's been secretly married to Lise these last four months. Her fortune and her good family connections make it impossible for me to annul the match. I've come to . . .

GORGIBUS. Say no more. If Valère has married someone else without permission, I must confess I promised my daughter to Lélie, who is endowed with many virtues. Since his return today, I wouldn't think of accepting anybody else for a son-in-law.

VILLEBREQUIN. I'm happy at the outcome.

LÉLIE (*to* GORGIBUS). By keeping your promise, you've made me the happiest man in the world.

GORGIBUS. Let's go and fix the day for the wedding.

SGANARELLE (*to the audience*). Have you ever seen such a self-deceived husband? In these matters, convincing evidence may lead to wrong conclusions. Therefore, even if you see everything, don't believe anything.

THE BEAR

A Joke in One Act
Dedicated to H. H. Solovitsov

by Anton Chekhov

WHEN at the age of twenty-eight Chekhov wrote *The Bear*, little did he suspect that he was producing the most successful and profitable play of his lifetime. Holding a low opinion of both the play and its performance, he was astonished at its popular success but gratified by its financial returns. "Having nothing to do, I wrote a silly little French vaudeville under the title of *The Bear*." Three months after its production he wrote, "My *Bear* should really be called the *Milchcow*. It has brought me more money than any of my short stories." Even Tolstoy, who criticized Chekhov because his *Sea Gull* and *Uncle Vanya* did not deal with social problems and their solution, "roared with laughter" at a performance of *The Bear*.

One act "vaudevilles" had been popular on the Russian stage for a century before Chekhov's time. For the most part, they are situation comedies with stock "humor" characters. Chekhov modified the genre by creating believable people. Nemirovich-Danchenko shrewdly explained the success of Chekhov's eight one act comedies in a single sentence: "The charm of these 'jokes' of his is due not only to their comic situations but also to the fact that their characters are living people and not stage vaudeville figures and that their dialogue is full of humor and characteristic dramatic surprises."

CHARACTERS

ELENA IVANOVNA POPOVA (a young widow with dimpled cheeks, landowner)
GRIGORY STEPANOVICH SMIRNOV (a middle-aged landowner)
LUKA (Popova's old servant)

The drawing room of POPOVA's *country home.*

(POPOVA, *in deep mourning, does not remove her eyes
from a photograph.*)

LUKA. It isn't right, madam . . . you're only destroy-
ing yourself . . . the chambermaid and the cook have
gone off berry picking, every living being is rejoicing;
even the cat knows how to be content, walking around
the yard catching birdies, and you sit in your room all
day as if it were a convent, and you don't take pleasure
in anything. Yes, really! Almost a year has passed since
you've gone out of the house!

POPOVA. And I shall never go out. . . . What for? My
life is already ended. He lies in his grave; I have buried
myself in these four walls . . . we are both dead.

LUKA. There you go again! Nikolai Mikhailovich is
dead, that's as it was meant to be, it's the will of God, may
he rest in peace. . . . You've done your mourning and
that will do. You can't go on weeping and mourning forever. My wife died when her time came, too. . . . Well?
I grieved, I wept for a month, and that was enough for
her; and if I had to weep like Lazarus, for four days, well,
the old lady just wasn't worth it. (*Sighs.*) You've forgotten all your neighbors. You don't go anywhere or accept
any calls. We live, so to speak, like spiders. We never see
the light. The mice have eaten my livery. It isn't as if
there weren't any nice neighbors—the district is full of
them . . . there's a regiment stationed at Riblov, such
officers—they're like bonbons—you'll never get your fill
of them! And in the barracks, never a Friday goes by
without a ball; and, if you please, the military band plays
music every day. . . . Yes, madam, my dear lady: you're
young, beautiful, in the full bloom of youth—if only you
took a little pleasure in life . . . beauty doesn't last for-

ever, you know! In ten years' time, you'll be wanting to spread your tail like a peahen in front of the officers—and it will be too late.

POPOVA (*determined*). I must ask you never to talk to me like that! You know that when Nikolai Mikhailovich died, life lost all its salt for me. It may seem to you that I am alive, but that's only conjecture! I vowed to wear mourning to my grave and not to see the light of day. . . . Do you hear me? May his departed spirit see how much I love him. . . . Yes, I know, it's no mystery to you that he was often mean to me, cruel . . . and even unfaithful, but I shall remain true to the grave and show him I know how to love. There, beyond the grave, he will see me as I was before his death. . . .

LUKA. Instead of talking like that, you should be taking a walk in the garden or have Toby or Giant harnessed and go visit some of the neighbors . . .

POPOVA. Ai! (*She weeps.*)

LUKA. Madam! Dear lady! What's the matter with you! Christ be with you!

POPOVA. Oh, how he loved Toby! He always used to ride on him to visit the Korchagins or the Vlasovs. How wonderfully he rode! How graceful he was when he pulled at the reins with all his strength! Do you remember? Toby, Toby! Tell them to give him an extra bag of oats today.

LUKA. Yes, madam.

(*Sound of loud ringing.*)

POPOVA (*shudders*). Who's that? Tell them I'm not at home!

LUKA. Of course, madam. (*He exits.*)

POPOVA (*alone. Looks at the photograph*). You will see, Nicholas, how much I can love and forgive . . . my love will die only when I do, when my poor heart stops beating. (*Laughing through her tears.*) Have you no shame? I'm a good girl, a virtuous little wife. I've locked myself in and I'll be true to you to the grave, and you . . . aren't you ashamed, you chubby cheeks? You deceived me, you made scenes, for weeks on end you left me alone . . .

LUKA (*enters, alarmed*). Madam, somebody is asking for you. He wants to see you. . . .

POPOVA. But didn't you tell them that since the death of my husband, I don't see anybody?

LUKA. I did, but he didn't want to listen; he spoke about some very important business.

POPOVA. I am *not at home!*

LUKA. That's what I told him . . . but . . . the devil . . . he cursed and pushed past me right into the room . . . he's in the dining room right now.

POPOVA (*losing her temper*). Very well, let him come in . . . such manners! (LUKA *goes out.*) How difficult these people are! What does he want from me? Why should he disturb my peace? (*Sighs.*) But it's obvious I'll have to go live in a convent. . . . (*Thoughtfully.*) Yes, a convent. . . .

SMIRNOV (*to* LUKA). You idiot, you talk too much. . . . Ass! (*Sees* POPOVA *and changes to dignified speech.*) Madam, may I introduce myself: retired lieutenant of the artillery and landowner, Grigory Stepanovich Smirnov! I feel the necessity of troubling you about a highly important matter. . . .

POPOVA (*refusing her hand*). What do you want?

SMIRNOV. Your late husband, whom I had the pleasure of knowing, has remained in my debt for two twelve-hundred-ruble notes. Since I must pay the interest at the agricultural bank tomorrow, I have come to ask you, madam, to pay me the money today.

POPOVA. One thousand two hundred. . . . And why was my husband in debt to you?

SMIRNOV. He used to buy oats from me.

POPOVA (*sighing, to* LUKA). So, Luka, don't you forget to tell them to give Toby an extra bag of oats.

(LUKA *goes out.*)

(*To* SMIRNOV.) If Nikolai Mikhailovich was in debt to you, then it goes without saying that I'll pay; but please excuse me today. I haven't any spare cash. The day after tomorrow, my steward will be back from town and I will give him instructions to pay you what is owed; until then I cannot comply with your wishes. . . . Besides, today is the anniversary—exactly seven months ago my husband died, and I'm in such a mood that I'm not quite disposed to occupy myself with money matters.

SMIRNOV. And I'm in such a mood that if I don't pay the interest tomorrow, I'll be owing so much that my troubles will drown me. They'll take away my estate!

POPOVA. You'll receive your money the day after tomorrow.

SMIRNOV. I don't want the money the day after tomorrow. I want it today.

POPOVA. You must excuse me. I can't pay you today.

SMIRNOV. And I can't wait until after tomorrow.

POPOVA. What can I do, if I don't have it now?

SMIRNOV. You mean to say you can't pay?

POPOVA. I can't pay. . . .

SMIRNOV. Hm! Is that your last word?

POPOVA. That is my last word.

SMIRNOV. Positively the last?

POPOVA. Positively.

SMIRNOV. Thank you very much. We'll make a note of that. (*Shrugs his shoulders.*) And people want me to be calm and collected! Just now, on the way here, I met a tax officer and he asked me: why are you always so angry, Grigory Stepanovich? Goodness' sake, how can I be anything but angry? I need money desperately . . . I rode out yesterday early in the morning, at daybreak, and went to see all my debtors; and if only one of them had paid his debt . . . I was dog-tired, spent the night God knows where—a Jewish tavern beside a barrel of vodka. . . . Finally I got here, fifty miles from home, hoping to be paid, and you treat me to a "mood." How can I help being angry?

POPOVA. It seems to me that I clearly said: My steward will return from the country and then you will be paid.

SMIRNOV. I didn't come to your steward, but to you! What the hell, if you'll pardon the expression, would I do with your steward?

POPOVA. Excuse me, my dear sir, I am not accustomed to such unusual expressions nor to such a tone. I'm not listening to you any more. (*Goes out quickly.*)

SMIRNOV (*alone*). Well, how do you like that? "A mood." . . . "Husband died seven months ago"! Must I pay the interest or mustn't I? I ask you: Must I pay, or must I not? So, your husband's dead, and you're in a mood and all that finicky stuff . . . and your steward's away somewhere, may he drop dead. What do you want me to do? Do you think I can fly away from my creditors in a balloon or something? Or should I run and bash my head against the wall? I go to Gruzdev—and he's not at home; Yaroshevich is hiding, with Kuritsin it's a quarrel to the death and I almost throw him out the window; Mazutov has diarrhea, and this one is in a "mood." Not one of these swine wants to pay me! And all because I'm too nice to them. I'm a sniveling idiot, I'm spineless, I'm an old lady! I'm too delicate with them! So, just you wait! You'll find out what I'm like! I won't let you play around with me, you devils! I'll stay and stick it out until she pays. Brr! . . . How furious I am today, how furious! I'm shaking inside from rage and I can hardly catch my breath. . . . Damn it! My God, I even feel sick! (*He shouts.*) Hey, you!

LUKA (*enters*). What do you want?

SMIRNOV. Give me some kvass or some water! (LUKA *exits.*) What logic is there in this! A man needs money desperately, it's like a noose around his neck—and she won't pay because, you see, she's not disposed to occupy herself with money matters! . . . That's the logic of a woman! That's why I never did like and do not like to talk to women. I'd rather sit on a keg of gunpowder than talk to a woman. Brr! . . . I even have goose pimples, this skirt has put me in such a rage! All I have to do is see one of those poetical creatures from a distance, and I get so angry it gives me a cramp in the leg. I just want to shout for help.

LUKA (*entering with water*). Madam is sick and won't see anyone.

SMIRNOV. Get out! (LUKA *goes.*) Sick and won't see anyone! No need to see me . . . I'll stay and sit here until you give me the money. You can stay sick for a week, and I'll stay for a week . . . if you're sick for a year, I'll stay a year. . . . I'll get my own back, dear lady! You can't impress me with your widow's weeds and your dimpled cheeks . . . we know all about those dimples! (*Shouts through the window.*) Semyon, unharness the horses! We're not going away quite yet! I'm staying here! Tell them in the stable to give the horses some oats! You brute, you let the horse on the left side get all tangled up in the reins again! (*Teasing.*) "Never mind" . . . I'll give you a never mind! (*Goes away from the window.*) Shit! The heat is unbearable and nobody pays up. I slept badly last night and on top of everything else this skirt in mourning is "in a mood" . . . my head aches . . . should I have some vodka? I wonder, should I? (*Shouts.*) Hey, you!

LUKA (*enters*). What is it?

SMIRNOV. Give me a glass of vodka. (LUKA *goes out.*) Oof! (*Sits down and examines himself.*) Nobody would say I was looking well! Dusty all over, boots dirty, unwashed, unkempt, straw on my waistcoat. . . . The dear lady probably took me for a robber. (*Yawns.*) It's not very polite to present myself in a drawing room looking like this; oh well, who cares? . . . I'm not here as a visitor but as a creditor, and there's no official costume for creditors. . . .

LUKA (*enters with vodka*). You're taking liberties, my good man. . . .

SMIRNOV (*angrily*). What?

LUKA. I . . . nothing . . . I only . . .

SMIRNOV. Who are you talking to? Shut up!

LUKA (*aside*). The devil sent this leech. An ill wind brought him. . . . (LUKA *goes out.*)

SMIRNOV. Oh how furious I am! I'm so mad I could crush the whole world into a powder! I even feel faint! (*Shouts.*) Hey, you!

POPOVA (*enters, eyes downcast*). My dear sir, in my

solitude, I have long ago grown unaccustomed to the masculine voice and I cannot bear shouting. I must request you not to disturb my peace and quiet!

SMIRNOV. Pay me my money and I'll go.

POPOVA. I told you in plain language: I haven't any spare cash now; wait until the day after tomorrow.

SMIRNOV. And I also told you respectfully, in plain language: I don't need the money the day after tomorrow, but today. If you don't pay me today, then tomorrow I'll have to hang myself.

POPOVA. But what can I do if I don't have the money? You're so strange!

SMIRNOV. Then you won't pay me now? No?

POPOVA. I can't. . . .

SMIRNOV. In that case, I can stay here and wait until you pay. . . . (*Sits down.*) You'll pay the day after tomorrow? Excellent! In that case I'll stay here until the day after tomorrow. I'll sit here all that time . . . (*Jumps up.*) I ask you: Have I got to pay the interest tomorrow, or not? Or do you think I'm joking?

POPOVA. My dear sir, I ask you not to shout! This isn't a stable!

SMIRNOV. I wasn't asking you about a stable but about this: do I have to pay the interest tomorrow or not?

POPOVA. You don't know how to behave in the company of a lady!

SMIRNOV. No, I don't know how to behave in the company of a lady!

POPOVA. No, you don't! You are an ill-bred, rude man! Respectable people don't talk to a woman like that!

SMIRNOV. Ach, it's astonishing! How would you like me to talk to you? In French, perhaps? (*Lisps in anger.*) *Madame, je vous prie* . . . how happy I am that you're not paying me the money. . . . Ah, pardon, I've made you uneasy! Such lovely weather we're having today! And you look so becoming in your mourning dress. (*Bows and scrapes.*)

POPOVA. That's rude and not very clever!

SMIRNOV (*teasing*). Rude and not very clever! I don't

know how to behave in the company of ladies. Madam, in my time I've seen far more women than you've seen sparrows. Three times I've fought duels over women; I've jilted twelve women, nine have jilted me! Yes! There was a time when I played the fool; I became sentimental over women, used honeyed words, fawned on them, bowed and scraped. . . . I loved, suffered, sighed at the moon; I became limp, melted, shivered . . . I loved passionately, madly, every which way, devil take me, I chattered away like a magpie about the emancipation of women, ran through half my fortune as a result of my tender feelings; but now, if you will excuse me, I'm on to your ways! I've had enough! Dark eyes, passionate eyes, ruby lips, dimpled cheeks; the moon, whispers, bated breath—for all that I wouldn't give a good goddamn. Present company excepted, of course, but all women, young and old alike, are affected clowns, gossips, hateful, consummate liars to the marrow of their bones, vain, trivial, ruthless, outrageously illogical, and as far as this is concerned (*Taps on his forehead.*), well, excuse my frankness, any sparrow could give pointers to a philosopher in petticoats! Look at one of those poetical creatures: muslin, ethereal demigoddess, a thousand raptures, and you look into her soul—a common crocodile! (*Grips the back of a chair; the chair cracks and breaks.*) But the most revolting part of it all is that this crocodile imagines that she has a chef d'oeuvre, her own privilege, a monopoly on tender feelings. The hell with it—you can hang me upside down by that nail if a woman is capable of loving anything besides a lapdog. All she can do when she's in love is slobber! While the man suffers and sacrifices, all her love is expressed in playing with her skirt and trying to lead him around firmly by the nose. You have the misfortune of being a woman, you know yourself what the nature of a woman is like. Tell me honestly: have you ever in your life seen a woman who is sincere, faithful, and constant? You never have! Only old and ugly ladies are faithful and constant! You're more liable to meet a horned cat or a white woodcock than a faithful woman!

POPOVA. Pardon me, but in your opinion, who is faithful and constant in love? The man?

SMIRNOV. Yes, the man!

POPOVA. The man! (*Malicious laugh.*) Men are faithful and constant in love! That's news! (*Heatedly.*) What right have you to say that? Men are faithful and constant! For that matter, as far as I know, of all the men I have known and now know, my late husband was the best. . . . I loved him passionately, with all my being, as only a young intellectual woman can love; I gave him my youth, my happiness, my life, my fortune; he was my life's breath; I worshiped him as if I were a heathen, and . . . and, what good did it do—this best of men himself deceived me shamelessly at every step of the way. After his death, I found his desk full of love letters; and when he was alive—it's terrible to remember—he used to leave me alone for weeks at a time, and before my very eyes he paid court to other women and deceived me. He squandered my money, made a mockery of my feelings . . . and, in spite of all that, I loved him and was true to him . . . and besides, now that he is dead, I am still faithful and constant. I have shut myself up in these four walls forever and I won't remove these widow's weeds until my dying day. . . .

SMIRNOV (*laughs contemptuously*). Widow's weeds! . . . I don't know what you take me for! As if I didn't know why you wear that black domino and bury yourself in these four walls! Well, well! It's so secret, so poetic! When a Junker or some fool of a poet passes by this country house, he'll look up at your window and think: "Here lives the mysterious Tamara, who, for the love of her husband, buried herself in these four walls." We know these tricks!

POPOVA (*flaring*). What? How dare you say that to me?

SMIRNOV. You may have buried yourself alive, but you haven't forgotten to powder yourself!

POPOVA. How dare you use such expressions with me?

SMIRNOV. Please don't shout. I'm not your steward! You must allow me to call a spade a spade. I'm not a

woman and I'm used to saying what's on my mind! Don't
you shout at me!

POPOVA. I'm not shouting, you are! Please leave me in
peace!

SMIRNOV. Pay me my money and I'll go.

POPOVA. I won't give you any money!

SMIRNOV. Yes, you will.

POPOVA. To spite you, I won't pay you anything. You
can leave me in peace!

SMIRNOV. I don't have the pleasure of being either your
husband or your fiancé, so please don't make scenes! (*Sits
down.*) I don't like it.

POPOVA (*choking with rage*). You're sitting down?

SMIRNOV. Yes, I am.

POPOVA. I ask you to get out!

SMIRNOV. Give me my money . . . (*Aside.*) Oh, I'm so
furious! Furious!

POPOVA. I don't want to talk to impudent people! Get
out of here! (*Pause.*) You're not going? No?

SMIRNOV. No.

POPOVA. No?

SMIRNOV. No!

POPOVA. Good for you! (*Rings.*)

    (LUKA *enters.*)
Luka, show the gentleman out!

LUKA (*goes up to* SMIRNOV). Sir, will you please leave,
as you have been asked. You mustn't . . .

SMIRNOV (*jumping up*). Shut up! Who do you think
you're talking to? I'll make mincemeat out of you!

LUKA (*his hand to his heart*). Oh my God! Saints
above! (*Falls into chair*). Oh, I feel ill! I feel ill! I can't
catch my breath!

POPOVA. Where's Dasha? Dasha! (*She shouts.*) Dasha!
Pelagea! Dasha! (*She rings.*)

LUKA. Oh! They've all gone berry picking . . . there's
nobody at home . . . I'm ill! Water!

POPOVA. Will you please get out!

SMIRNOV. Will you please be more polite?

POPOVA (*clenches her fist and stamps her feet*). You're a muzhik! You're a crude bear! A brute! A monster!

SMIRNOV. What? What did you say?

POPOVA. I said that you were a bear, a monster!

SMIRNOV (*advancing toward her*). Excuse me, but what right do you have to insult me?

POPOVA. Yes, I am insulting you . . . so what? Do you think I'm afraid of you?

SMIRNOV. And do you think just because you're one of those poetical creatures, that you have the right to insult me with impunity? Yes? I challenge you!

LUKA. Lord in Heaven! Saints above! . . . Water!

SMIRNOV. Pistols!

POPOVA. Do you think just because you have big fists and you can bellow like a bull, that I'm afraid of you? You're such a bully!

SMIRNOV. I challenge you! I'm not going to let anybody insult me, and I don't care if you are a woman, a fragile creature!

POPOVA (*trying to get a word in edgewise*). Bear! Bear! Bear!

SMIRNOV. It's about time we got rid of the prejudice that only men must pay for their insults! Devil take it, if women want to be equal, they should behave as equals! Let's fight!

POPOVA. You want to fight! By all means!

SMIRNOV. This minute!

POPOVA. This minute! My husband had some pistols . . . I'll go and get them right away. (*Goes out hurriedly and then returns.*) What pleasure I'll have putting a bullet through that thick head of yours! The hell with you! (*She goes out.*)

SMIRNOV. I'll shoot her down like a chicken! I'm not a little boy or a sentimental puppy. Fragile creatures don't exist for me.

LUKA. Kind sir! Holy father! (*Kneels.*) Have pity on a poor old man and go away from here! You've frightened her to death and now you're going to shoot her?

SMIRNOV (*not listening to him*). If she fights, then it

means she believes in equality of rights and the emancipation of women. Here the sexes are equal! I'll shoot her like a chicken! But what a woman! (*Imitates her.*) "The hell with you! . . . I'll put a bullet through that thick head of yours! . . ." What a woman! How she blushed, her eyes shone . . . she accepted my challenge! To tell the truth, it was the first time in my life I've seen a woman like that. . . .

LUKA. Dear sir, please go away! I'll pray to God on your behalf as long as I live!

SMIRNOV. That's a woman for you! A woman like that I can understand! A real woman! Not a sour-faced nincompoop but fiery, gunpowder! Fireworks! I'm even sorry to have to kill her!

LUKA (*weeps*). Dear sir . . . go away!

SMIRNOV. I positively like her! Positively! Even though she has dimpled cheeks, I like her! I'm almost ready to forget about the debt. . . . My fury has diminished. Wonderful woman!

POPOVA (*enters with pistols*). Here they are, the pistols. Before we fight, you must show me how to fire. . . . I've never had a pistol in my hands before . . .

LUKA. Oh dear Lord, for pity's sake. . . . I'll go and find the gardener and the coachman. . . . What did we do to deserve such trouble? (*Exits.*)

SMIRNOV (*examining the pistols*). You see, there are several sorts of pistols . . . there are special dueling pistols, the Mortimer with primers. Then there are Smith and Wesson revolvers, triple action with extractors . . . excellent pistols! . . . they cost a minimum of ninety rubles a pair. . . . You must hold the revolver like this . . . (*Aside.*) What eyes, what eyes! A woman to set you on fire!

POPOVA. Like this?

SMIRNOV. Yes, like this . . . then you cock the pistol . . . take aim . . . put your head back a little . . . stretch your arm out all the way . . . that's right . . . then with this finger press on this little piece of goods . . . and that's all there is to do . . . but the most important

thing is not to get excited and aim without hurrying . . .
try to keep your arm from shaking.

POPOVA. Good . . . it's not comfortable to shoot indoors. Let's go into the garden.

SMIRNOV. Let's go. But I'm giving you advance notice
that I'm going to fire into the air.

POPOVA. That's the last straw! Why?

SMIRNOV. Why? . . . Why . . . because it's my business, that's why.

POPOVA. Are you afraid? Yes? Aahhh! No, sir. You're
not going to get out of it that easily! Be so good as to fol-
low me! I will not rest until I've put a hole through your
forehead . . . that forehead I hate so much! Are you
afraid?

SMIRNOV. Yes, I'm afraid.

POPOVA. You're lying! Why don't you want to fight?

SMIRNOV. Because . . . because you . . . because I
like you.

POPOVA (*laughs angrily*). He likes me! He dares say
that he likes me! (*Points to the door.*) Out!

SMIRNOV (*loads the revolver in silence, takes cap and
goes; at the door, stops for half a minute while they look
at each other in silence; then he approaches* POPOVA *hesi-
tantly*). Listen. . . . Are you still angry? I'm extremely
irritated, but, do you understand me, how can I express
it . . . the fact is, that, you see, strictly speaking . . .
(*He shouts.*) Is it my fault, really, for liking you? (*Grabs
the back of a chair; chair cracks and breaks.*) Why the
hell do you have such fragile furniture! I like you! Do
you understand? I . . . I'm almost in love with you!

POPOVA. Get away from me—I hate you!

SMIRNOV. God, what a woman! I've never in my life
seen anything like her! I'm lost! I'm done for! I'm caught
like a mouse in a trap!

POPOVA. Stand back or I'll shoot!

SMIRNOV. Shoot! You could never understand what happiness it would be to die under the gaze of those wonderful eyes, to be shot by a revolver which was held by those
little velvet hands. . . . I've gone out of my mind! Think

about it and decide right away, because if I leave here, then we'll never see each other again! Decide . . . I'm a nobleman, a respectable gentleman, of good family. I have an income of ten thousand a year. . . . I can put a bullet through a coin tossed in the air . . . I have some fine horses. . . . Will you be my wife?

POPOVA (*indignantly brandishes her revolver*). Let's fight! I challenge you!

SMIRNOV. I'm out of my mind . . . I don't understand anything . . . (*Shouts.*) Hey, you, water!

POPOVA (*shouts*). Let's fight!

SMIRNOV. I've gone out of my mind. I'm in love like a boy, like an idiot! (*He grabs her hand, she screams with pain.*) I love you! (*Kneels.*) I love you as I've never loved before! I've jilted twelve women, nine women have jilted me, but I've never loved one of them as I love you. . . . I'm weak, I'm a limp rag . . . I'm on my knees like a fool, offering you my hand. . . . Shame, shame! I haven't been in love for five years, I vowed I wouldn't; and suddenly I'm in love, like a fish out of water. I'm offering my hand in marriage. Yes or no? You don't want to? You don't need to! (*Gets up and quickly goes to the door.*)

POPOVA. Wait!

SMIRNOV (*stops*). Well?

POPOVA. Nothing . . . you can go . . . go away . . . wait. . . . No, get out, get out! I hate you! But— Don't go! Oh, if you only knew how furious I am, how angry! (*Throws revolver on table.*) My fingers are swollen from that nasty thing. . . . (*Tears her handkerchief furiously.*) What are you waiting for? Get out!

SMIRNOV. Farewell!

POPOVA. Yes, yes, go away! (*Shouts.*) Where are you going? Stop. . . . Oh, go away! Oh, how furious I am! Don't come near me! Don't come near me!

SMIRNOV (*approaching her*). How angry I am with myself! I'm in love like a student, I've been on my knees. . . . It gives me the shivers. (*Rudely.*) I love you! A lot of good it will do me to fall in love with you! Tomorrow I've got to pay the interest, begin the mowing of the hay.

(*Puts his arm around her waist.*) I'll never forgive myself
for this. . . .

POPOVA. Get away from me! Get your hands away! I
. . . hate you! I . . . challenge you!

> (*Prolonged kiss.* LUKA *enters with an ax, the* GAR-
> DENER *with a rake, the* COACHMAN *with a pitchfork,
> and* WORKMEN *with cudgels.*)

LUKA (*catches sight of the pair kissing*). Lord in heav-
en! (*Pause.*)

POPOVA (*lowering her eyes*). Luka, tell them in the stable not to give Toby any oats today.

CURTAIN

HOW HE LIED
TO HER HUSBAND

by George Bernard Shaw

TAKING ADVANTAGE of four days of continuous rain during a holiday in the north of Scotland in 1904, Shaw wrote *How He Lied to Her Husband.* It was Shaw's second play on an age-old theme. Ten years before, he had written *Candida,* a play with a similar rationalistic and anti-romantic attitude toward the conventional domestic love triangle.

In *Candida,* the realistic wife forces her deluded mate to see his true position as a coddled, pampered husband who needs her protection. At the same time, she helps the romantic young poet discover his destiny as an independent, alienated artist capable of facing the hardships and rebuffs of a cruel world. In *How He Lied to Her Husband,* it is the sensible husband who precipitates the revelation of the true character of the wife, and the folly of the lover. Although the marriages are preserved in both plays, the endings are very different for the poets. In *Candida* the youthful Marchbanks, rejecting bourgeois domestic happiness, impatiently flies out into the night to meet his destiny, while here poor Apjohn is left ruefully brooding over his discomfiture. Although *How He Lied to Her Husband* lacks *Candida*'s depth of characterization and social satire, it is noteworthy for broad farcical elements.

CHARACTERS

HER LOVER (Apjohn)
HER HUSBAND (Bompas)
HERSELF (Aurora Bompas)

It is eight o'clock in the evening. The curtains are drawn
and the lamps lighted in the drawing room of Her flat in
Cromwell Road. Her lover, a beautiful youth of eighteen,
in evening dress and cape, with a bunch of flowers and an
opera hat in his hands, comes in alone. The door is near
the corner; and as he appears in the doorway, he has the
fireplace on the nearest wall to his right, and the grand
piano along the opposite wall to his left. Near the fireplace a small ornamental table has on it a hand mirror, a
fan, a pair of long white gloves, and a little white woollen
cloud to wrap a woman's head in. On the other side of the
room, near the piano, is a broad, square, softly upholstered
stool. The room is furnished in the most approved South
Kensington fashion: that is, it is as like a shop window as
possible, and is intended to demonstrate the social position
and spending powers of its owners, and not in the least to
make them comfortable.

He is, be it repeated, a very beautiful youth, moving as
in a dream, walking as on air. He puts his flowers down
carefully on the table beside the fan; takes off his cape,
and, as there is no room on the table for it, takes it to the
piano; puts his hat on the cape; crosses to the hearth;
looks at his watch; puts it up again; notices the things on
the table; lights up as if he saw heaven opening before
him; goes to the table and takes the cloud in both hands,
nestling his nose into its softness and kissing it; kisses the
gloves one after another; kisses the fan; gasps a long
shuddering sigh of ecstasy; sits down on the stool and
presses his hands to his eyes to shut out reality and dream
a little; takes his hands down and shakes his head with
a little smile of rebuke for his folly; catches sight of a
speck of dust on his shoes and hastily and carefully

44

brushes it off with his handkerchief; rises and takes the hand mirror from the table to make sure of his tie with the gravest anxiety; and is looking at his watch again when She comes in, much flustered. As she is dressed for the theatre; has spoilt, petted ways; and wears many diamonds, she has an air of being a young and beautiful woman; but as a matter of hard fact, she is, dress and pretensions apart, a very ordinary South Kensington female of about thirty seven, hopelessly inferior in physical and spiritual distinction to the beautiful youth, who hastily puts down the mirror as she enters.

HE [*kissing her hand*] At last!

SHE. Henry: something dreadful has happened.

HE. Whats the matter?

SHE. I have lost your poems.

HE. They were unworthy of you. I will write you some more.

SHE. No, thank you. Never any more poems for me. Oh, how could I have been so mad! so rash! so imprudent!

HE. Thank Heaven for your madness, your rashness, your imprudence!

SHE [*impatiently*] Oh, be sensible, Henry. Cant you see what a terrible thing this is for me? Suppose anybody finds these poems! what will they think?

HE. They will think that a man once loved a woman more devotedly than ever man loved woman before. But they will not know what man it was.

SHE. What good is that to me if everybody will know what woman it was?

HE. But how will they know?

SHE. How will they know! Why, my name is all over them: my silly, unhappy name. Oh, if I had only been christened Mary Jane, or Gladys Muriel, or Beatrice, or Francesca, or Guinevere, or something quite common! But Aurora! Aurora! I'm the only Aurora in London; and everybody knows it. I believe I'm the only Aurora in the world. And it's so horribly easy to rhyme to it! Oh, Henry, why didnt you try to restrain your feelings a little in common consideration for me? Why didnt you write with some little reserve?

HE. Write poems to you with reserve! You ask me that!

SHE [*with perfunctory tenderness*] Yes, dear, of course it was very nice of you; and I know it was my own fault as much as yours. I ought to have noticed that your verses ought never to have been addressed to a married woman.

HE. Ah, how I wish they had been addressed to an unmarried woman! how I wish they had!

SHE. Indeed you have no right to wish anything of the sort. They are quite unfit for anybody but a married woman. Thats just the difficulty. What will my sisters-in-law think of them?

HE [*painfully jarred*] Have you got sisters-in-law?

SHE. Yes, of course I have. Do you suppose I am an angel?

HE [*biting his lips*] I do. Heaven help me, I do—or I did—or [*he almost chokes a sob*].

SHE [*softening and putting her hand caressingly on his shoulder*] Listen to me, dear. It's very nice of you to live with me in a dream, and to love me, and so on; but I cant help my husband having disagreeable relatives, can I?

HE [*brightening up*] Ah, of course they are your husband's relatives: I forgot that. Forgive me, Aurora. [*He takes her hand from his shoulder and kisses it. She sits down on the stool. He remains near the table, with his back to it, smiling fatuously down at her*].

SHE. The fact is, Teddy's got nothing but relatives. He has eight sisters and six half-sisters, and ever so many brothers—but I dont mind his brothers. Now if you only knew the least little thing about the world, Henry, youd know that in a large family, though the sisters quarrel with one another like mad all the time, yet let one of the brothers marry, and they all turn on their unfortunate sister-in-law and devote the rest of their lives with perfect unanimity to persuading him that his wife is unworthy of him. They can do it to her very face without her knowing it, because they always have a lot of stupid low family jokes that nobody understands but themselves.

Half the time you cant tell what theyre talking about: it just drives you wild. There ought to be a law against a man's sister ever entering his house after he's married. I'm as certain as that I'm sitting here that Georgina stole those poems out of my workbox.

HE. She will not understand them, I think.

SHE. Oh, wont she! She'll understand them only too well. She'll understand more harm than ever was in them: nasty vulgar-minded cat!

HE [*going to her*] Oh dont, dont think of people in that way. Dont think of her at all. [*He takes her hand and sits down on the carpet at her feet*]. Aurora: do you remember the evening when I sat here at your feet and read you those poems for the first time?

SHE. I shouldnt have let you: I see that now. When I think of Georgina sitting there at Teddy's feet and reading them to him for the first time, I feel I shall just go distracted.

HE. Yes, you are right. It will be a profanation.

SHE. Oh, I dont care about the profanation; but what will Teddy think? what will he do? [*Suddenly throwing his head away from her knee*] You dont seem to think a bit about Teddy. [*She jumps up, more and more agitated*].

HE [*supine on the floor; for she has thrown him off his balance*] To me Teddy is nothing, and Georgina less than nothing.

SHE. Youll soon find out how much less than nothing she is. If you think a woman cant do any harm because she's only a scandalmongering dowdy ragbag, youre greatly mistaken. [*She flounces about the room. He gets up slowly and dusts his hands. Suddenly she runs to him and throws herself into his arms*]. Henry: help me. Find a way out of this for me; and I'll bless you as long as you live. Oh, how wretched I am! [*She sobs on his breast*].

HE. And oh! how happy I am!

SHE [*whisking herself abruptly away*] Dont be selfish.

HE [*humbly*] Yes: I deserve that. I think if I were going to the stake with you, I should still be so happy with you that I should forget your danger as utterly as my own.

SHE [*relenting and patting his hand fondly*] Oh, you
are a dear darling boy, Henry; but [*throwing his hand
away fretfully*] youre no use. I want somebody to tell me
what to do.

HE [*with quiet conviction*] Your heart will tell you at
the right time. I have thought deeply over this; and I
know what we two must do, sooner or later.

SHE. No, Henry. I will do nothing improper, nothing
dishonorable. [*She sits down plump on the stool and looks
inflexible*].

HE. If you did, you would no longer be Aurora. Our
course is perfectly simple, perfectly straightforward, perfectly stainless and true. We love one another. I am not
ashamed of that: I am ready to go out and proclaim it to
all London as simply as I will declare it to your husband
when you see—as you soon will see—that this is the only
way honorable enough for your feet to tread. Let us go
out together to our own house, this evening, without con-
cealment and without shame. Remember! we owe something to your husband. We are his guests here: he is an
honorable man: he has been kind to us: he has perhaps
loved you as well as his prosaic nature and his sordid commercial environment permitted. We owe it to him in all
honor not to let him learn the truth from the lips of a scan-
dalmonger. Let us go to him now quietly, hand in hand;
bid him farewell; and walk out of the house without con-
cealment or subterfuge, freely and honestly, in full honor
and self-respect.

SHE [*staring at him*] And where shall we go to?

HE. We shall not depart by a hair's breadth from the
ordinary natural current of our lives. We were going to
the theatre when the loss of the poems compelled us to
take action at once. We shall go to the theatre still; but
we shall leave your diamonds here; for we cannot afford
diamonds, and do not need them.

SHE [*fretfully*] I have told you already that I hate diamonds; only Teddy insists on hanging me all over with
them. You need not preach simplicity to me.

HE. I never thought of doing so, dearest: I know that these trivialities are nothing to you. What was I saying?—oh yes. Instead of coming back here from the theatre, you will come with me to my home—now and henceforth our home—and in due course of time, when you are divorced, we shall go through whatever idle legal ceremony you may desire. *I* attach no importance to the law; my love was not created in me by the law, nor can it be bound or loosed by it. That is simple enough, and sweet enough, is it not? [*He takes the flowers from the table*]. Here are flowers for you: I have the tickets: we will ask your husband to lend us the carriage to shew that there is no malice, no grudge, between us. Come!

SHE. Do you mean to say that you propose that we should walk right bang up to Teddy and tell him we're going away together?

HE. Yes. What can be simpler?

SHE. And do you think for a moment he'd stand it? He'd just kill you.

HE [*coming to a sudden stop and speaking with considerable confidence*] You dont understand these things, my darling: how could you? I have followed the Greek ideal and not neglected the culture of my body. Like all poets I have a passion for pugilism. Your husband would make a tolerable second-rate heavy weight if he were in training and ten years younger. As it is, he could, if strung up to a great effort by a burst of passion, give a good account of himself for perhaps fifteen seconds. But I am active enough to keep out of his reach for fifteen seconds; and after that I should be simply all over him.

SHE [*rising and coming to him in consternation*] What do you mean by all over him?

HE [*gently*] Dont ask me, dearest. At all events, I swear to you that you need not be anxious about me.

SHE. And what about Teddy? Do you mean to tell me that you are going to beat Teddy before my face like a brutal prizefighter?

HE. All this alarm is needless, dearest. Believe me, nothing will happen. Your husband knows that I am capable of defending myself. Under such circumstances nothing ever does happen. And of course *I* shall do nothing. The man who once loved you is sacred to me.

SHE [*suspiciously*] Doesnt he love me still? Has he told you anything?

HE. No, no. [*He takes her tenderly in his arms*]. Dearest, dearest: how agitated you are! how unlike yourself! All these worries belong to the lower plane. Come up with me to the higher one. The heights, the solitudes, the soul world!

SHE [*avoiding his gaze*] No: stop: it's no use, Mr Apjohn.

HE [*recoiling*] Mr Apjohn!!!

SHE. Excuse me: I meant Henry, of course.

HE. How could you even think of me as Mr Apjohn? I never think of you as Mrs Bompas: it is always Aurora, Aurora, Auro—

SHE. Yes, yes: thats all very well, Mr Apjohn [*he is about to interrupt again: but she wont have it*] no: it's no use: Ive suddenly begun to think of you as Mr Apjohn; and it's ridiculous to go on calling you Henry. I thought you were only a boy, a child, a dreamer. I thought you would be too much afraid to do anything. And now you want to beat Teddy and to break up my home and disgrace me and make a horrible scandal in the papers. It's cruel, unmanly, cowardly.

HE [*with grave wonder*] Are you afraid?

SHE. Oh, of course I'm afraid. So would you be if you had any common sense. [*She goes to the hearth, turning her back to him, and puts one tapping foot on the fender*].

HE [*watching her with great gravity*] Perfect love casteth out fear. That is why I am not afraid. Mrs Bompas: you do not love me.

SHE [*turning to him with a gasp of relief*] Oh, thank you, thank you! You really can be very nice, Henry.

HE. Why do you thank me?

SHE [*coming prettily to him from the fireplace*] For calling me Mrs Bompas again. I feel now that you are going to be reasonable and behave like a gentleman. [*He *drops on the stool; covers his face with his hands; and groans*]. Whats the matter?

HE. Once or twice in my life I have dreamed that I was exquisitely happy and blessed. But oh! the misgiving at the first stir of consciousness! the stab of reality! the prison walls of the bedroom! the bitter, bitter disappointment of waking! And this time! oh, this time I thought I was awake.

SHE. Listen to me, Henry: we really havnt time for all that sort of flapdoodle now. [*He starts to his feet as if she had pulled a trigger and straightened him by the release of a powerful spring, and goes past her with set teeth to the little table*]. Oh, take care: you nearly hit me in the chin with the top of your head.

HE [*with fierce politeness*] I beg your pardon. What is it you want me to do? I am at your service. I am ready to behave like a gentleman if you will be kind enough to explain exactly how.

SHE [*a little frightened*] Thank you, Henry: I was sure you would. Youre not angry with me, are you?

HE. Go on. Go on quickly. Give me something to think about, or I will—I will—[*he suddenly snatches up her fan and is about to break it in his clenched fist*].

SHE [*running forward and catching at the fan, with loud lamentation*] Dont break my fan—no, dont. [*He slowly relaxes his grip of it as she draws it anxiously out of his hands*]. No, really, thats a stupid trick: I dont like that. Youve no right to do that. [*She opens the fan, and finds that the sticks are disconnected*]. Oh, how could you be so inconsiderate?

HE. I beg your pardon. I will buy you a new one.

SHE [*querulously*] You will never be able to match it. And it was a particular favorite of mine.

HE [*shortly*] Then you will have to do without it: thats all.

SHE. Thats not a very nice thing to say after breaking my pet fan, I think.

HE. If you knew how near I was to breaking Teddy's pet wife and presenting him with the pieces, you would be thankful that you are alive instead of—of—of howling about fiveshillings-worth of ivory. Damn your fan!

SHE. Oh! Dont you dare swear in my presence. One would think you were my husband.

HE [*again collapsing on the stool*] This is some horrible dream. What has become of you? You are not my Aurora.

SHE. Oh, well, if you come to that, what has become of you? Do you think I would ever have encouraged you if I had known you were such a little devil?

HE. Dont drag me down—dont—dont. Help me to find the way back to the heights.

SHE [*kneeling beside him and pleading*] If you would only be reasonable, Henry. If you would only remember that I am on the brink of ruin, and not go on calmly saying it's all quite simple.

HE. It seems so to me.

SHE [*jumping up distractedly*] If you say that again I shall do something I'll be sorry for. Here we are, standing on the edge of a frightful precipice. No doubt it's quite simple to go over and have done with it. But cant you suggest anything more agreeable?

HE. I can suggest nothing now. A chill black darkness has fallen: I can see nothing but the ruins of our dream. [*He rises with a deep sigh*].

SHE. Cant you? Well, I can. I can see Georgina rubbing those poems into Teddy. [*Facing him determinedly*] And I tell you, Henry Apjohn, that you got me into this mess; and you must get me out of it again.

HE [*polite and hopeless*] All I can say is that I am entirely at your service. What do you wish me to do?

SHE. Do you know anybody else named Aurora?

HE. No.

SHE. Theres no use in saying No in that frozen pig-headed way. You must know some Aurora or other somewhere.

HE. You said you were the only Aurora in the world. And [*lifting his clasped fists with a sudden return of his emotion*] oh God! you were the only Aurora in the world for me. [*He turns away from her, hiding his face*].

SHE [*petting him*] Yes, yes, dear: of course. It's very nice of you; and I appreciate it: indeed I do; but it's not seasonable just at present. Now just listen to me. I suppose you know all those poems by heart.

HE. Yes, by heart. [*Raising his head and looking at her with a sudden suspicion*] Dont you?

SHE. Well, I never can remember verses; and besides, Ive been so busy that Ive not had time to read them all; though I intend to the very first moment I can get: I promise you that most faithfully, Henry. But now try and remember very particularly. Does the name of Bompas occur in any of the poems?

HE [*indignantly*] No.

SHE. Youre quite sure?

HE. Of course I am quite sure. How could I use such a name in a poem?

SHE. Well, I dont see why not. It rhymes to rumpus, which seems appropriate enough at present, goodness knows! However, youre a poet, and you ought to know.

HE. What does it matter—now?

SHE. It matters a lot, I can tell you. If theres nothing about Bompas in the poems, we can say that they were written to some other Aurora, and that you shewed them to me because my name was Aurora too. So youve got to invent another Aurora for the occasion.

HE [*very coldly*] Oh, if you wish me to tell a lie—

SHE. Surely, as a man of honor—as a gentleman, you wouldnt tell the truth: would you?

HE. Very well. You have broken my spirit and desecrated my dreams. I will lie and protest and stand on my honor: oh, I will play the gentleman, never fear.

SHE. Yes, put it all on me, of course. Dont be mean, Henry.

HE [*rousing himself with an effort*] You are quite right, Mrs. Bompas: I beg your pardon. You must excuse my temper. I am having growing pains, I think.

SHE. Growing pains!

HE. The process of growing from romantic boyhood into cynical maturity usually takes fifteen years. When it is compressed into fifteen minutes, the pace is too fast; and growing pains are the result.

SHE. Oh, is this a time for cleverness? It's settled, isnt it, that youre going to be nice and good, and that youll brazen it out to Teddy that you have some other Aurora?

HE. Yes: I'm capable of anything now. I should not have told him the truth by halves; and now I will not lie by halves. I'll wallow in the honor of a gentleman.

SHE. Dearest boy, I knew you would. I—Sh! [*She rushes to the door, and holds it ajar, listening breathlessly*].

HE. What is it?

SHE [*white with apprehension*] It's Teddy: I hear him tapping the new barometer. He cant have anything serious on his mind or he wouldnt do that. Perhaps Georgina hasnt said anything. [*She steals back to the hearth*]. Try and look as if there was nothing the matter. Give me my gloves, quick. [*He hands them to her. She pulls on one hastily and begins buttoning it with ostentatious unconcern*]. Go further away from me, quick. [*He walks doggedly away from her until the piano prevents his going farther*]. If I button my glove, and you were to hum a tune, dont you think that—

HE. The tableau would be complete in its guiltiness. For Heaven's sake, Mrs Bompas, let that glove alone: you look like a pickpocket.

> *Her husband comes in: a robust, thicknecked, well groomed city man, with a strong chin but a blithering eye and credulous mouth. He has a momentous air, but shews no sign of displeasure: rather the contrary.*

HER HUSBAND. Hallo! I thought you two were at the theatre.

SHE. I felt anxious about you, Teddy. Why didnt you come home to dinner?

HER HUSBAND. I got a message from Georgina. She wanted me to go to her.

SHE. Poor dear Georgina! I'm sorry I havnt been able

to call on her this last week. I hope theres nothing the matter with her.

HER HUSBAND. Nothing, except anxiety for my welfare —and yours. [*She steals a terrified look at* HENRY]. By the way, Apjohn, I should like a word with you this evening, if Aurora can spare you for a moment.

HE [*formally*] I am at your service.

HER HUSBAND. No hurry. After the theatre will do.

HE. We have decided not to go.

HER HUSBAND. Indeed! Well, then, shall we adjourn to my snuggery?

SHE. You neednt move. I shall go and lock up my diamonds since I'm not going to the theatre. Give me my things.

HER HUSBAND [*as he hands her the cloud and the mirror*] Well, we shall have more room here.

HE [*looking about him and shaking his shoulders loose*] I think I should prefer plenty of room.

HER HUSBAND. So, if it's not disturbing you, Rory—?

SHE. Not at all. [*She goes out*].

When the two men are alone together, BOMPAS *deliberately takes the poems from his breast pocket; looks at them reflectively; then looks at* HENRY, *mutely inviting his attention.* HENRY *refuses to understand, doing his best to look unconcerned.*

HER HUSBAND. Do these manuscripts seem at all familiar to you, may I ask?

HE. Manuscripts?

HER HUSBAND. Yes. Would you like to look at them a little closer? [*He proffers them under* HENRY'*s nose*].

HE [*as with a sudden illumination of glad surprise*] Why, these are my poems!

HER HUSBAND. So I gather.

HE. What a shame! Mrs Bompas has shewn them to you! You must think me an utter ass. I wrote them years ago after reading Swinburne's Songs Before Sunrise. Nothing would do me then but I must reel off a set of Songs to the Sunrise. Aurora, you know: the rosy fingered Aurora. Theyre all about Aurora. When Mrs Bompas told me her

name was Aurora, I couldnt resist the temptation to lend
them to her to read. But I didn't bargain for your unsym-
pathetic eyes.

HER HUSBAND [*grinning*] Apjohn: thats really very
ready of you. You are cut out for literature; and the day
will come when Rory and I will be proud to have you
about the house. I have heard far thinner stories from
much older men.

HE [*with an air of great surprise*] Do you mean to im-
ply that you dont believe me?

HER HUSBAND. Do you expect me to believe you?

HE. Why not? I dont understand.

HER HUSBAND. Come! Dont underrate your own cleverness, Apjohn. I think you understand pretty well.

HE. I assure you I am quite at a loss. Can you not be a
little more explicit?

HER HUSBAND. Dont overdo it, old chap. However, I
will just be so far explicit as to say that if you think these
poems read as if they were addressed, not to a live woman, but to a shivering cold time of day at which you were
never out of bed in your life, you hardly do justice to your
own literary powers—which I admire and appreciate, mind
you, as much as any man. Come! own up. You wrote those
poems to my wife. [*An internal struggle prevents* HENRY
from answering]. Of course you did. [*He throws the poems
on the table; and goes to the hearthrug, where he plants
himself solidly, chuckling a little and waiting for the next
move*].

HE [*formally and carefully*] Mr Bompas: I pledge you
my word you are mistaken. I need not tell you that Mrs
Bompas is a lady of stainless honor, who has never cast
an unworthy thought on me. The fact that she has shewn
you my poems—

HER HUSBAND. Thats not a fact. I came by them without her knowledge. She didnt shew them to me.

HE. Does not that prove their perfect innocence? She
would have shewn them to you at once if she had taken
your quite unfounded view of them.

HER HUSBAND [*shaken*] Apjohn: play fair. Dont abuse

your intellectual gifts. Do you really mean that I am making a fool of myself?

HE [*earnestly*] Believe me, you are. I assure you, on my honor as a gentleman, that I have never had the slightest feeling for Mrs. Bompas beyond the ordinary esteem and regard of a pleasant acquaintance.

HER HUSBAND [*shortly, shewing ill humor for the first time*] Oh! Indeed! [*He leaves his hearth and begins to approach* HENRY *slowly, looking him up and down with growing resentment*].

HE [*hastening to improve the impression made by his mendacity*] I should never have dreamt of writing poems to her. The thing is absurd.

HER HUSBAND [*reddening ominously*] Why is it absurd?

HE [*shrugging his shoulders*] Well, it happens that I do not admire Mrs Bompas—in that way.

HER HUSBAND [*breaking out in* HENRY's *face*] Let me tell you that Mrs Bompas has been admired by better men than you, you soapy h̀aded little puppy, you.

HE [*much taken aback*] There is no need to insult me like this. I assure you, on my honor as a—

HER HUSBAND [*too angry to tolerate a reply, and boring* HENRY *more and more towards the piano*] You dont admire Mrs Bompas! You would never dream of writing poems to Mrs Bompas! My wife's not good enough for you, isnt she? [*Fiercely*] Who are you, pray, that you should be so jolly superior?

HE. Mr Bompas: I can make allowances for your jealousy—

HER HUSBAND. Jealousy! do you suppose I'm jealous of you? No, nor of ten like you. But if you think I'll stand here and let you insult my wife in her own house, youre mistaken.

HE [*very uncomfortable with his back against the piano and* TEDDY *standing over him threateningly*] How can I convince you? Be reasonable. I tell you my relations with Mrs Bompas are relations of perfect coldness—of indifference—

HER HUSBAND [*scornfully*] Say it again: say it again.

Youre proud of it, arnt you? Yah! youre not worth kick-
ing.

> HENRY *suddenly executes the feat known to pugil-*
> *ists as slipping, and changes sides with* TEDDY, *who is*
> *now between* HENRY *and the piano.*

HE. Look here: I'm not going to stand this.

HER HUSBAND. Oh, you have some blood in your body
after all! Good job!

HE. This is ridiculous. I assure you Mrs Bompas is
quite—

HER HUSBAND. What is Mrs Bompas to you, I'd like to
know. I'll tell you what Mrs Bompas is. She's the smartest woman in the smartest set in South Kensington, and
the handsomest, and the cleverest, and the most fetching
to experienced men who know a good thing when they see
it, whatever she may be to conceited penny-a-lining pup-
pies who think nothing good enough for them. It's admitted by the best people; and not to know it argues yourself
unknown. Three of our first actor-managers have offered
her a hundred a week if she'll go on the stage when they
start a repertory theatre; and I think they know what
theyre about as well as you. The only member of the present Cabinet that you might call a handsome man has neglected the business of the country to dance with her,
though he dont belong to our set as a regular thing. One
of the first professional poets in Bedford Park wrote a
sonnet to her, worth all your amateur trash. At Ascot last
season the eldest son of a duke excused himself from calling on me on the ground that his feelings for Mrs Bompas were not consistent with his duty to me as host; and
it did him honor and me too. But [*with gathering fury*]
she isnt good enough for you, it seems. You regard her
with coldness, with indifference; and you have the cool
cheek to tell me so to my face. For two pins I'd flatten
your nose in to teach you manners. Introducing a fine
woman to you is casting pearls before swine [*yelling at*
him] before SWINE! d'ye hear?

HE [*with a deplorable lack of polish*] You call me a

swine again and I'll land you one on the chin thatll make
your head sing for a week.

HER HUSBAND [*exploding*] What!

> *He charges at* HENRY *with bull-like fury.* HENRY
> *places himself on guard in the manner of a well taught
> boxer, and gets away smartly, but unfortunately for-
> gets the stool which is just behind him. He falls back-
> wards over it, unintentionally pushing it against the
> shins of* BOMPAS, *who falls forward over it.* MRS BOM-
> PAS, *with a scream, rushes into the room between the
> sprawling champions, and sits down on the floor in
> order to get her right arm round her husband's neck.*

SHE. You shant, Teddy: you shant. You will be killed:
he is a prizefighter.

HER HUSBAND [*vengefully*] I'll prizefight him. [*He
struggles vainly to free himself from her embrace*].

SHE. Henry: dont let him fight you. Promise me that
you wont.

HE [*ruefully*] I have got a most frightful bump on the
back of my head. [*He tries to rise*].

SHE [*reaching out her left hand to seize his coat tail,
and pulling him down again, whilst keeping fast hold of
TEDDY with the other hand*] Not until you have promised:
not until you both have promised. [TEDDY *tries to rise:
she pulls him back again*]. Teddy: you promise, dont
you? Yes, yes. Be good: you promise.

HER HUSBAND. I wont, unless he takes it back.

SHE. He will: he does. You take it back, Henry?—yes.

HE [*savagely*] Yes. I take it back. [*She lets go his coat.
He gets up. So does* TEDDY]. I take it all back, all, without reserve.

SHE [*on the carpet*] Is nobody going to help me up?
[*They each take a hand and pull her up*]. Now wont you
shake hands and be good?

HE [*recklessly*] I shall do nothing of the sort. I have
steeped myself in lies for your sake; and the only reward
I get is a lump on the back of my head the size of an apple.
Now I will go back to the straight path.

SHE. Henry: for Heaven's sake—

HE. It's no use. Your husband is a fool and a brute—

HER HUSBAND. Whats that you say?

HE. I say you are a fool and a brute; and if youll step outside with me I'll say it again. [TEDDY *begins to take off his coat for combat*]. Those poems were written to your wife, every word of them, and to nobody else. [*The scowl clears away from* BOMPAS'S *countenance. Radiant, he replaces his coat*]. I wrote them because I loved her. I thought her the most beautiful woman in the world, and I told her so over and over again. I adored her: do you hear? I told her that you were a sordid commercial chump, utterly unworthy of her; and so you are.

HER HUSBAND [*so gratified, he can hardly believe his ears*] You dont mean it!

HE. Yes, I do mean it, and a lot more too. I asked Mrs Bompas to walk out of the house with me—to leave you —to get divorced from you and marry me. I begged and implored her to do it this very night. It was her refusal that ended everything between us. [*Looking very disparagingly at him*] What she can see in you, goodness only knows!

HER HUSBAND [*beaming with remorse*] My dear chap, why didnt you say so before? I apologize. Come! dont bear malice: shake hands. Make him shake hands, Rory.

SHE. For my sake, Henry. After all, he's my husband. Forgive him. Take his hand. [HENRY, *dazed, lets her take his hand and place it in* TEDDY'S].

HER HUSBAND [*shaking it heartily*] Youve got to own that none of your literary heroines can touch my Rory. [*He turns to her and clasps her with fond pride on the shoulders*]. Eh, Rory? They cant resist you: none of em. Never knew a man yet that could hold out three days.

SHE. Dont be foolish, Teddy. I hope you were not really hurt, Henry. [*She feels the back of his head. He flinches*]. Oh, poor boy, what a bump! I must get some vinegar and brown paper. [*She goes to the bell and rings*].

HER HUSBAND. Will you do me a great favor, Apjohn. I hardly like to ask; but it would be a real kindness to us both.

HE. What can I do?

HER HUSBAND [*taking up the poems*] Well, may I get these printed? It shall be done in the best style. The finest paper, sumptuous binding, everything first class. Theyre beautiful poems. I should like to shew them about a bit.

SHE [*running back from the bell, delighted with the idea, and coming between them*] Oh Henry, if you wouldnt mind?

HE. Oh, *I* dont mind. I am past minding anything.

HER HUSBAND. What shall we call the volume? To Aurora, or something like that, eh?

HE. I should call it How He Lied to Her Husband.

SPREADING THE NEWS

by Lady Gregory

THE YEARS Lady Gregory spent visiting the country people in her neighborhood gathering folklore stood her in good stead when she came to write *Spreading the News*. Her sympathetic attitude and impeccable memory helped her to capture the authentic accents and speech rhythms of the Irish common people. In addition to her talent for picturesque dialogue, she possessed a vivid power of characterization, a keen sense of satire, and a firm grasp of theatrical action. In *Spreading the News, The Gaol Gate* (1906), *The Workhouse Ward* (1907), and *Hyacinth Halvey* (1907), she created a series of Irish genre paintings surpassed only by the plays of Synge.

CHARACTERS

BARTLEY FALLON
MRS. FALLON
JACK SMITH
SHAWN EARLY
TIM CASEY
JAMES RYAN

MRS. TARPEY
MRS. TULLY
A POLICEMAN (Jo Muldoon)
A REMOVABLE MAGISTRATE

SCENE: *The outskirts of a Fair. An Apple Stall.*

(MRS. TARPEY *sitting at it.* MAGISTRATE *and* POLICE-
MAN *enter.*)

MAGISTRATE. So that is the Fair Green. Cattle and sheep
and mud. No system. What a repulsive sight!

POLICEMAN. That is so, indeed.

MAGISTRATE. I suppose there is a good deal of disorder
in this place?

POLICEMAN. There is.

MAGISTRATE. Common assault.

POLICEMAN. It's common enough.

MAGISTRATE. Agrarian crime, no doubt?

POLICEMAN. That is so.

MAGISTRATE. Boycotting? Maiming of cattle? Firing
into houses?

POLICEMAN. There was one time, and there might be
again.

MAGISTRATE. That is bad. Does it go any farther than
that?

POLICEMAN. Far enough, indeed.

MAGISTRATE. Homicide, then! This district has been
shamefully neglected! I will change all that. When I was
in the Andaman Islands, my system never failed. Yes, yes,
I will change all that. What has that woman on her stall?

POLICEMAN. Apples mostly—and sweets.

MAGISTRATE. Just see if there are any unlicensed goods
underneath—spirits or the like. We had evasions of the
salt tax in the Andaman Islands.

POLICEMAN (*sniffing cautiously and upsetting a heap of
apples*). I see no spirits here—or salt.

MAGISTRATE (*to* MRS. TARPEY). Do you know this town
well, my good woman?

66

MRS. TARPEY (*holding out some apples*). A penny the half-dozen, your honour.

POLICEMAN (*shouting*). The gentleman is asking do you know the town? He's the new magistrate!

MRS. TARPEY (*rising and ducking*). Do I know the town? I do, to be sure.

MAGISTRATE (*shouting*). What is its chief business?

MRS. TARPEY. Business, is it? What business would the people here have but to be minding one another's business?

MAGISTRATE. I mean what trade have they?

MRS. TARPEY. Not a trade. No trade at all but to be talking.

MAGISTRATE. I shall learn nothing here.

(JAMES RYAN *comes in, pipe in mouth. Seeing* MAGISTRATE *he retreats quickly, taking pipe from mouth.*)
The smoke from that man's pipe had a greenish look; he may be growing unlicensed tobacco at home. I wish I had brought my telescope to this district. Come to the post-office, I will telegraph for it. I found it very useful in the Andaman Islands.

(MAGISTRATE *and* POLICEMAN *go out left.*)

MRS. TARPEY. Bad luck to Jo Muldoon, knocking my apples this way and that way. (*Begins arranging them.*) Showing off he was to the new magistrate.

(*Enter* BARTLEY FALLON *and* MRS. FALLON.)

BARTLEY. Indeed it's a poor country and a scarce country to be living in. But I'm thinking if I went to America it's long ago the day I'd be dead!

MRS. FALLON. So you might, indeed. (*She puts her basket on a barrel and begins putting parcels in it, taking them from under her cloak.*)

BARTLEY. And it's a great expense for a poor man to be buried in America.

MRS. FALLON. Never fear, Bartley Fallon, but I'll give you a good burying the day you'll die.

BARTLEY. Maybe it's yourself will be buried in the graveyard of Cloonmara before me, Mary Fallon, and I myself that will be dying unbeknownst some night, and no one a-near me. And the cat itself may be gone straying through the country, and the mice squealing over the quilt.

MRS. FALLON. Leave off talking of dying. It might be twenty years you'll be living yet.

BARTLEY (*with a deep sigh*). I'm thinking if I'll be living at the end of twenty years, it's a very old man I'll be then!

MRS. TARPEY (*turns and sees them*). Good morrow, Bartley Fallon; good morrow, Mrs. Fallon. Well, Bartley, you'll find no cause for complaining today; they are all saying it was a good fair.

BARTLEY (*raising his voice*). It was not a good fair, Mrs. Tarpey. It was a scattered sort of a fair. If we didn't expect more, we got less. That's the way with me always; whatever I have to sell goes down and whatever I have to buy goes up. If there's ever any misfortune coming to this world, it's on myself it pitches, like a flock of crows on seed potatoes.

MRS. FALLON. Leave off talking of misfortunes, and listen to Jack Smith that is coming the way, and he singing.

(*Voice of* JACK SMITH *heard singing*):

I thought, my first love,
    There'd be but one house between you and me,
And I thought I would find
    Yourself coaxing my child on your knee.
Over the tide
    I would leap with the leap of a swan,
Till I came to the side
    Of the wife of the red-haired man!

(JACK SMITH *comes in; he is a red-haired man, and is carrying a hayfork.*)

MRS. TARPEY. That should be a good song if I had my hearing.

MRS. FALLON (*shouting*). It's "The Red-haired Man's Wife."

MRS. TARPEY. I know it well. That's the song that has a skin on it! (*She turns her back to them and goes on arranging her apples.*)

MRS. FALLON. Where's herself, Jack Smith?

JACK SMITH. She was delayed with her washing; bleaching the clothes on the hedge she is, and she daren't leave them, with all the tinkers that do be passing to the fair. It isn't to the fair I came myself, but up to the Five Acre Meadow I'm going, where I have a contract for the hay. We'll get a share of it into tramps today. (*He lays down hayfork and lights his pipe.*)

BARTLEY. You will not get it into tramps today. The rain will be down on it by evening, and on myself too. It's seldom I ever started on a journey but the rain would come down on me before I'd find any place of shelter.

JACK SMITH. If it didn't itself, Bartley, it is my belief you would carry a leaky pail on your head in place of a hat, the way you'd not be without some cause for complaining.

(*A voice heard, "Go on, now, go on out o' that. Go on I say."*)
Look at that young mare of Pat Ryan's that is backing into Shaughnessy's bullocks with the dint of the crowd! Don't be daunted, Pat, I'll give you a hand with her. (*He goes out, leaving his hayfork.*)

MRS. FALLON. It's time for ourselves to be going home. I have all I bought put in the basket. Look at there, Jack Smith's hayfork he left after him! He'll be wanting it. (*Calls.*) Jack Smith! Jack Smith!—He's gone through the crowd—hurry after him, Bartley, he'll be wanting it.

BARTLEY. I'll do that. This is no safe place to be leaving it. (*He takes up fork awkwardly and upsets the basket.*) Look at that now! If there is any basket in the fair upset, it must be our own basket! (*He goes out to right.*)

MRS. FALLON. Get out of that! It is your own fault, it is. Talk of misfortunes and misfortunes will come. Glory be! Look at my new egg-cups rolling in every part—and my two pound of sugar with the paper broke—

MRS. TARPEY (*turning from stall*). God help us, Mrs. Fallon, what happened to your basket?

MRS. FALLON. It's himself that knocked it down, bad manners to him. (*Putting things up.*) My grand sugar that's destroyed, and he'll not drink his tea without it. I had best go back to the shop for more, much good may it do him!

(*Enter* TIM CASEY.)

TIM CASEY. Where is Bartley Fallon, Mrs. Fallon? I want a word with him before he'll leave the fair. I was afraid he might have gone home by this, for he's a temperate man.

MRS. FALLON. I wish he did go home! It'd be best for me if he went home straight from the fair green, or if he never came with me at all! Where is he, is it? He's gone up the road (*Jerks elbow.*) following Jack Smith with a hayfork. (*She goes out to left.*)

TIM CASEY. Following Jack Smith with a hayfork! Did ever any one hear the like of that. (*Shouts.*) Did you hear that news, Mrs. Tarpey?

MRS. TARPEY. I heard no news at all.

TIM CASEY. Some dispute I suppose it was that rose between Jack Smith and Bartley Fallon, and it seems Jack made off, and Bartley is following him with a hayfork!

MRS. TARPEY. Is he now? Well, that was quick work! It's not ten minutes since the two of them were here, Bartley going home and Jack going to the Five Acre Meadow; and I had my apples to settle up, that Jo Muldoon of the police had scattered, and when I looked round again Jack Smith was gone, and Bartley Fallon was gone, and Mrs. Fallon's basket upset, and all in it strewed upon the ground—the tea here—the two pound of sugar there—the egg-cups there— Look, now, what a great hardship the deafness puts upon me, that I didn't hear the commincement of the fight! Wait till I tell James Ryan that I see below; he is a neighbour of Bartley's, it would be a pity if he wouldn't hear the news!

(*She goes out. Enter* SHAWN EARLY *and* MRS. TULLY.)

TIM CASEY. Listen, Shawn Early! Listen, Mrs. Tully, to the news! Jack Smith and Bartley Fallon had a falling out, and Jack knocked Mrs. Fallon's basket into the road, and Bartley made an attack on him with a hayfork, and away with Jack, and Bartley after him. Look at the sugar here yet on the road!

SHAWN EARLY. Do you tell me so? Well, that's a queer thing, and Bartley Fallon so quiet a man!

MRS. TULLY. I wouldn't wonder at all. I would never think well of a man that would have that sort of a mouldering look. It's likely he has overtaken Jack by this.

(*Enter* JAMES RYAN *and* MRS. TARPEY.)

JAMES RYAN. That is great news Mrs. Tarpey was telling me! I suppose that's what brought the police and the magistrate up this way. I was wondering to see them in it a while ago.

SHAWN EARLY. The police after them? Bartley Fallon must have injured Jack so. They wouldn't meddle in a fight that was only for show!

MRS. TULLY. Why wouldn't he injure him? There was many a man killed with no more of a weapon than a hayfork.

JAMES RYAN. Wait till I run north as far as Kelly's bar to spread the news! (*He goes out.*)

TIM CASEY. I'll go tell Jack Smith's first cousin that is standing there south of the church after selling his lambs. (*Goes out.*)

MRS. TULLY. I'll go telling a few of the neighbours I see beyond to the west. (*Goes out.*)

SHAWN EARLY. I'll give word of it beyond at the east of the green. (*Is going out when* MRS. TARPEY *seizes hold of him.*)

MRS. TARPEY. Stop a minute, Shawn Early, and tell me did you see red Jack Smith's wife, Kitty Keary, in any place?

SHAWN EARLY. I did. At her own house she was, drying clothes on the hedge as I passed.

MRS. TARPEY. What did you say she was doing?

SHAWN EARLY (*breaking away*). Laying out a sheet on the hedge. (*He goes.*)

MRS. TARPEY. Laying out a sheet for the dead! The Lord have mercy on us! Jack Smith dead, and his wife laying out a sheet for his burying! (*Calls out.*) Why didn't you tell me that before, Shawn Early? Isn't the deafness the great hardship? Half the world might be dead without me knowing of it or getting word of it at all! (*She sits down and rocks herself.*) O my poor Jack Smith! To be going to his work so nice and so hearty, and to be left stretched on the ground in the full light of the day!

(*Enter* TIM CASEY.)

TIM CASEY. What is it, Mrs. Tarpey? What happened since?

MRS. TARPEY. O my poor Jack Smith!

TIM CASEY. Did Bartley overtake him?

MRS. TARPEY. O the poor man!

TIM CASEY. Is it killed he is?

MRS. TARPEY. Stretched in the Five Acre Meadow!

TIM CASEY. The Lord have mercy on us! Is that a fact?

MRS. TARPEY. Without the rites of the Church or a ha'porth!

TIM CASEY. Who was telling you?

MRS. TARPEY. And the wife laying out a sheet for his corpse. (*Sits up and wipes her eyes.*) I suppose they'll wake him the same as another?

(*Enter* MRS. TULLY, SHAWN EARLY, *and* JAMES RYAN.)

MRS. TULLY. There is great talk about this work in every quarter of the fair.

MRS. TARPEY. Ochone! cold and dead. And myself maybe the last he was speaking to!

JAMES RYAN. The Lord save us! Is it dead he is?

TIM CASEY. Dead surely, and his wife getting provision for the wake.

SHAWN EARLY. Well, now, hadn't Bartley Fallon great venom in him?

MRS. TULLY. You may be sure he had some cause. Why would he have made an end of him if he had not? (*To* MRS. TARPEY, *raising her voice.*) What was it rose the dispute at all, Mrs. Tarpey?

MRS. TARPEY. Not a one of me knows. The last I saw of them, Jack Smith was standing there, and Bartley Fallon was standing there, quiet and easy, and he listening to "The Red-haired Man's Wife."

MRS. TULLY. Do you hear that, Tim Casey? Do you hear that, Shawn Early and James Ryan? Bartley Fallon was here this morning listening to red Jack Smith's wife, Kitty Keary that was! Listening to her and whispering with her! It was she started the fight so!

SHAWN EARLY. She must have followed him from her own house. It is likely some person roused him.

TIM CASEY. I never knew, before, Bartley Fallon was great with Jack Smith's wife.

MRS. TULLY. How would you know it? Sure it's not in the streets they would be calling it. If Mrs. Fallon didn't know of it, and if I that have the next house to them didn't know of it, and if Jack Smith himself didn't know of it, it is not likely you would know of it, Tim Casey.

SHAWN EARLY. Let Bartley Fallon take charge of her from this out so, and let him provide for her. It is little pity she will get from any person in this parish.

TIM CASEY. How can he take charge of her? Sure he has a wife of his own. Sure you don't think he'd turn souper and marry her in a Protestant church?

JAMES RYAN. It would be easy for him to marry her if he brought her to America.

SHAWN EARLY. With or without Kitty Keary, believe me it is for America he's making at this minute. I saw the new magistrate and Jo Muldoon of the police going into the post-office as I came up—there was hurry on them— you may be sure it was to telegraph they went, the way he'll be stopped in the docks at Queenstown!

MRS. TULLY. It's likely Kitty Keary is gone with him, and not minding a sheet or a wake at all. The poor man, to be deserted by his own wife, and the breath hardly gone out yet from his body that is lying bloody in the field!

(*Enter* MRS. FALLON.)

MRS. FALLON. What is it the whole of the town is talking about? And what is it you yourselves are talking about? Is it about my man Bartley Fallon you are talking? Is it lies about him you are telling, saying that he went killing Jack Smith? My grief that ever he came into this place at all!

JAMES RYAN. Be easy now, Mrs. Fallon. Sure there is no one at all in the whole fair but is sorry for you!

MRS. FALLON. Sorry for me, is it? Why would any one be sorry for me? Let you be sorry for yourselves, and that there may be shame on you for ever and at the day of judgment, for the words you are saying and the lies you are telling to take away the character of my poor man, and to take the good name off of him, and to drive him to destruction! That is what you are doing!

SHAWN EARLY. Take comfort now, Mrs. Fallon. The police are not so smart as they think. Sure he might give them the slip yet, the same as Lynchehaun.

MRS. TULLY. If they do get him, and if they do put a rope around his neck, there is no one can say he does not deserve it!

MRS. FALLON. Is that what you are saying, Bridget Tully, and is that what you think? I tell you it's too much talk you have, making yourself out to be such a great one, and to be running down every respectable person! A rope, is it? It isn't much of a rope was needed to tie up your own furniture the day you came into Martin Tully's house, and you never bringing as much as a blanket, or a penny, or a suit of clothes with you and I myself bringing seventy pounds and two feather beds. And now you are stiffer than a woman would have a hundred pounds! It is too much talk the whole of you have. A rope is it? I tell you the whole of this town is full of liars and schemers that would hang you up for half a glass of whisky. (*Turning to go.*) People they are you wouldn't believe as much as daylight from without you'd get up to have a look at it yourself. Killing Jack Smith indeed! Where are you at all, Bartley, till I bring you out of this? My nice quiet little man! My decent comrade! He that is as kind and as harmless as an innocent beast of the field! He'll be doing no harm at all if he'll shed the blood of some of you after this day's work! That much would be no harm at all.

(*Calls out.*) Bartley! Bartley Fallon! Where are you? (*Going out.*) Did any one see Bartley Fallon?

(*All turn to look after her.*)

JAMES RYAN. It is hard for her to believe any such a thing, God help her!

(*Enter* BARTLEY FALLON *from right, carrying hayfork.*)

BARTLEY. It is what I often said to myself, if there is ever any misfortune coming to this world it is on myself it is sure to come!

(*All turn around and face him.*)

To be going about with this fork and to find no one to take it, and no place to leave it down, and I wanting to be gone out of this— Is that you, Shawn Early? (*Holds out fork.*) It's well I met you. You have no call to be leaving the fair for a while the way I have, and how can I go till I'm rid of this fork? Will you take it and keep it until such time as Jack Smith—

SHAWN EARLY (*backing*). I will not take it, Bartley Fallon, I'm very thankful to you!

BARTLEY (*turning to apple stall*). Look at it now, Mrs. Tarpey, it was here I got it; let me thrust it in under the stall. It will lie there safe enough, and no one will take notice of it until such time as Jack Smith—

MRS. TARPEY. Take your fork out of that! Is it to put trouble on me and to destroy me you want? putting it there for the police to be rooting it out maybe. (*Thrusts him back.*)

BARTLEY. That is a very unneighbourly thing for you to do, Mrs. Tarpey. Hadn't I enough care on me with that fork before this, running up and down with it like the swinging of a clock, and afeard to lay it down in any place! I wish I never touched it or meddled with it at all!

JAMES RYAN. It is a pity, indeed, you ever did.

BARTLEY. Will you yourself take it, James Ryan? You were always a neighbourly man.

JAMES RYAN (*backing*). There is many a thing I would do for you, Bartley Fallon, but I won't do that!

SHAWN EARLY. I tell you there is no man will give you

any help or any encouragement for this day's work. If it was something agrarian now—

BARTLEY. If no one at all will take it, maybe it's best to give it up to the police.

TIM CASEY. There'd be a welcome for it with them surely! (*Laughter.*)

MRS. TULLY. And it is to the police Kitty Keary herself will be brought.

MRS. TARPEY (*rocking to and fro*). I wonder now who will take the expense of the wake for poor Jack Smith?

BARTLEY. The wake for Jack Smith!

TIM CASEY. Why wouldn't he get a wake as well as another? Would you begrudge him that much?

BARTLEY. Red Jack Smith dead! Who was telling you?

SHAWN EARLY. The whole town knows of it by this.

BARTLEY. Do they say what way did he die?

JAMES RYAN. You don't know that yourself, I suppose, Bartley Fallon? You don't know he was followed and that he was laid dead with the stab of a hayfork?

BARTLEY. The stab of a hayfork!

SHAWN EARLY. You don't know, I suppose, that the body was found in the Five Acre Meadow?

BARTLEY. The Five Acre Meadow!

TIM CASEY. It is likely you don't know that the police are after the man that did it?

BARTLEY. The man that did it?

MRS. TULLY. You don't know, maybe, that he was made away with for the sake of Kitty Keary, his wife?

BARTLEY. Kitty Keary, his wife! (*Sits down bewildered.*)

MRS. TULLY. And what have you to say now, Bartley Fallon?

BARTLEY (*crossing himself*). I to bring that fork here, and to find that news before me! It is much if I can ever stir from this place at all, or reach as far as the road!

TIM CASEY. Look, boys, at the new magistrate, and Jo Muldoon along with him! It's best for us to be quit this.

SHAWN EARLY. That is so. It is best not to be mixed in this business at all.

JAMES RYAN. Bad as he is, I wouldn't like to be an informer against any man.

(*All hurry away except* MRS. TARPEY, *who remains behind her stall. Enter* MAGISTRATE *and* POLICEMAN.)

MAGISTRATE. I knew the district was in a bad state, but I did not expect to be confronted with a murder at the first fair I came to.

POLICEMAN. I am sure you did not, indeed.

MAGISTRATE. It was well I had not gone home. I caught a few words here and there that roused my suspicions.

POLICEMAN. So they would, too.

MAGISTRATE. You heard the same story from everyone you asked?

POLICEMAN. The same story—or if it was not altogether the same, anyway it was no less than the first story.

MAGISTRATE. What is that man doing? He is sitting alone with a hayfork. He has a guilty look. The murder was done with a hayfork!

POLICEMAN (*in a whisper*). That's the very man they say did the act; Bartley Fallon himself!

MAGISTRATE. He must have found escape difficult—he is trying to brazen it out. A convict in the Andaman Islands tried the same game, but he could not escape my system! Stand aside— Don't go far— Have the handcuffs ready. (*He walks up to* BARTLEY, *folds his arms, and stands before him.*) Here, my man, do you know anything of John Smith?

BARTLEY. Of John Smith! Who is he, now?

POLICEMAN. Jack Smith, sir—Red Jack Smith!

MAGISTRATE (*coming a step nearer and tapping him on the shoulder*). Where is Jack Smith?

BARTLEY (*with a deep sigh, and shaking his head slowly*). Where is he, indeed?

MAGISTRATE. What have you to tell?

BARTLEY. It is where he was this morning, standing in this spot, singing his share of songs—no, but lighting his pipe—scraping a match on the sole of his shoe—

MAGISTRATE. I ask you, for the third time, where is he?

BARTLEY. I wouldn't like to say that. It is a great mystery, and it is hard to say of any man, did he earn hatred or love.

MAGISTRATE. Tell me all you know.

BARTLEY. All that I know— Well, there are the three estates; there is Limbo, and there is Purgatory, and there is—

MAGISTRATE. Nonsense! This is trifling! Get to the point.

BARTLEY. Maybe you don't hold with the clergy so? That is the teaching of the clergy. Maybe you hold with the old people. It is what they do be saying, that the shadow goes wandering, and the soul is tired, and the body is taking a rest— The shadow! (*Starts up.*) I was nearly sure I saw Jack Smith not ten minutes ago at the corner of the forge, and I lost him again— Was it his ghost I saw, do you think?

MAGISTRATE (*to* POLICEMAN). Conscience-struck! He will confess all now!

BARTLEY. His ghost to come before me! It is likely it was on account of the fork! I do have it and he to have no way to defend himself the time he met with his death!

MAGISTRATE (*to* POLICEMAN). I must note down his words. (*Takes out notebook. To* BARTLEY.) I warn you that your words are being noted.

BARTLEY. If I had ha' run faster in the beginning, this terror would not be on me at the latter end! Maybe he will cast it up against me at the day of judgment—I wouldn't wonder at all at that.

MAGISTRATE (*writing*). At the day of judgment—

BARTLEY. It was soon for his ghost to appear to me—is it coming after me always by day it will be, and stripping the clothes off in the night time?—I wouldn't wonder at all at that, being as I am an unfortunate man!

MAGISTRATE (*sternly*). Tell me this truly. What was the motive of this crime?

BARTLEY. The motive, is it?

MAGISTRATE. Yes; the motive; the cause.

BARTLEY. I'd sooner not say that.

MAGISTRATE. You had better tell me truly. Was it money?

BARTLEY. Not at all! What did poor Jack Smith ever have in his pockets unless it might be his hands that would be in them?

MAGISTRATE. Any dispute about land?

BARTLEY (*indignantly*). Not at all! He never was a grabber or grabbed from any one!

MAGISTRATE. You will find it better for you if you tell me at once.

BARTLEY. I tell you I wouldn't for the whole world wish to say what it was—it is a thing I would not like to be talking about.

MAGISTRATE. There is no use in hiding it. It will be discovered in the end.

BARTLEY. Well, I suppose it will, seeing that mostly everybody knows it before. Whisper here now. I will tell no lie; where would be the use? (*Puts his hand to his mouth, and* MAGISTRATE *stoops.*) Don't be putting the blame on the parish, for such a thing was never done in the parish before—it was done for the sake of Kitty Keary, Jack Smith's wife.

MAGISTRATE (*to* POLICEMAN). Put on the handcuffs. We have been saved some trouble. I knew he would confess if taken in the right way.

(POLICEMAN *puts on handcuffs.*)

BARTLEY. Handcuffs now! Glory be! I always said, if there was ever any misfortune coming to this place it was on myself it would fall. I to be in handcuffs! There's no wonder at all in that.

(*Enter* MRS. FALLON, *followed by the rest. She is looking back at them as she speaks.*)

MRS. FALLON. Telling lies the whole of the people of this town are; telling lies, telling lies as fast as a dog will trot! Speaking against my poor respectable man! Saying he made an end of Jack Smith! My decent comrade! There is no better man and no kinder man in the whole of the five parishes! It's little annoyance he ever gave to any one! (*Turns and sees him.*) What in the earthly world do I see before me? Bartley Fallon in charge of the police! Handcuffs on him! O Bartley, what did you do at all at all?

BARTLEY. O Mary, there has a great misfortune come upon me! It is what I always said, that if there is ever any misfortune—

MRS. FALLON. What did he do at all, or is it bewitched I am?

MAGISTRATE. This man has been arrested on a charge of murder.

MRS. FALLON. Whose charge is that? Don't believe them! They are all liars in this place! Give me back my man!

MAGISTRATE. It is natural that you should take his part, but you have no cause of complaint against your neighbours. He has been arrested for the murder of John Smith, on his own confession.

MRS. FALLON. The saints of heaven protect us! And what did he want killing Jack Smith?

MAGISTRATE. It is best you should know all. He did it on account of a love affair with the murdered man's wife.

MRS. FALLON (*sitting down*). With Jack Smith's wife! With Kitty Keary!—Ochone, the traitor!

THE CROWD. A great shame, indeed. He is a traitor, indeed.

MRS. TULLY. To America he was bringing her, Mrs. Fallon.

BARTLEY. What are you saying, Mary? I tell you—

MRS. FALLON. Don't say a word! I won't listen to any word you'll say! (*Stops her ears.*) O, isn't he the treacherous villain? Ochone go deo!

BARTLEY. Be quiet till I speak! Listen to what I say!

MRS. FALLON. Sitting beside me on the ass car coming to the town, so quiet and so respectable, and treachery like that in his heart!

BARTLEY. Is it your wits you have lost or is it I myself that have lost my wits?

MRS. FALLON. And it's hard I earned you, slaving, slaving—and you grumbling, and sighing, and coughing, and discontented, and the priest wore out anointing you, with all the times you threatened to die!

BARTLEY. Let you be quiet till I tell you!

MRS. FALLON. You to bring such a disgrace into the parish. A thing that was never heard of before!

BARTLEY. Will you shut your mouth and hear me speaking?

MRS. FALLON. And if it was for any sort of a fine handsome woman, but for a little fistful of a woman like Kitty Keary, that's not four feet high hardly, and not three teeth in her head unless she got new ones! May God reward you, Bartley Fallon, for the black treachery in your heart and the wickedness in your mind, and the red blood of poor Jack Smith that is wet upon your hand!

(*Voice of* JACK SMITH *heard singing*):

> The sea shall be dry.
> The earth under mourning and ban!
> Then loud shall he cry
> For the wife of the red-haired man!

BARTLEY. It's Jack Smith's voice—I never knew a ghost to sing before— It is after myself and the fork he is coming! (*Goes back. Enter* JACK SMITH.) Let one of you give him the fork and I will be clear of him now and for eternity!

MRS. TARPEY. The Lord have mercy on us! Red Jack Smith! The man that was going to be waked!

JAMES RYAN. Is it back from the grave you are come?

SHAWN EARLY. Is it alive you are, or is it dead you are?

TIM CASEY. Is it yourself at all that's in it?

MRS. TULLY. Is it letting on you were to be dead?

MRS. FALLON. Dead or alive, let you stop Kitty Keary, your wife, from bringing my man away with her to America!

JACK SMITH. It is what I think, the wits are gone astray on the whole of you. What would my wife want bringing Bartley Fallon to America?

MRS. FALLON. To leave yourself, and to get quit of you she wants, Jack Smith, and to bring him away from myself. That's what the two of them had settled together.

JACK SMITH. I'll break the head of any man that says that! Who is it says it? (*To* TIM CASEY.) Was it you said it? (*To* SHAWN EARLY.) Was it you?

ALL TOGETHER (*backing and shaking their heads*). It wasn't I said it!

JACK SMITH. Tell me the name of any man that said it!

ALL TOGETHER (*pointing to* BARTLEY). It was *him* that said it!

JACK SMITH. Let me at him till I break his head!

(BARTLEY *backs in terror. Neighbours hold* JACK SMITH *back.*)

(*Trying to free himself.*) Let me at him! Isn't he the pleasant sort of a scarecrow for any woman to be crossing the ocean with! It's back from the docks of New York he'd be turned (*Trying to rush at him again.*), with a lie in his mouth and treachery in his heart, and another man's wife by his side, and he passing her off as his own! Let me at him can't you. (*Makes another rush, but is held back.*)

MAGISTRATE (*pointing to* JACK SMITH). Policeman, put the handcuffs on this man. I see it all now. A case of false impersonation, a conspiracy to defeat the ends of justice. There was a case in the Andaman Islands, a murderer of the Mopsa tribe, a religious enthusiast—

POLICEMAN. So he might be, too.

MAGISTRATE. We must take both these men to the scene of the murder. We must confront them with the body of the real Jack Smith.

JACK SMITH. I'll break the head of any man that will find my dead body!

MAGISTRATE. I'll call more help from the barracks. (*Blows* POLICEMAN'S *whistle.*)

BARTLEY. It is what I am thinking, if myself and Jack Smith are put together in the one cell for the night, the handcuffs will be taken off him, and his hands will be free, and murder will be done that time surely!

MAGISTRATE. Come on! (*They turn to the right.*)

Author's Note

THE IDEA of this play first came to me as a tragedy. I kept seeing as in a picture people sitting by the roadside, and a girl passing to the market, gay and fearless. And then I saw her passing by the same place at evening, her head hanging, the heads of others turned from her, because of some sudden story that had risen out of a chance word, and had snatched away her good name.

But comedy and not tragedy was wanted at our theater to put beside the high poetic work, *The King's Threshold, The Shadowy Waters, On Baile's Strand, The Well of the Saints;* and I let laughter have its way with the little play. I was delayed in beginning it for a while, because I could only think of Bartley Fallon as dull-witted or silly or ignorant, and the handcuffs seemed too harsh a punishment. But one day by the seat at Duras a melancholy man who was telling me of the crosses he had gone through at home said —"But I'm thinking if I went to America, it's long ago today I'd be dead. And it's a great expense for a poor man to be buried in America." Bartley was born at that moment, and, far from harshness, I felt I was providing him with a happy old age in giving him the lasting glory of that great and crowning day of misfortune.

It has been acted very often by other companies as well as our own, and the Boers have done me the honor of translating and pirating it.

RIDERS TO THE SEA

by John M. Synge

SINCE ITS PRODUCTION in 1904 *Riders to the Sea* has remained on its lonely pinnacle as the unrivaled one act tragic masterpiece. In depicting the fatalistic resignation of a bereaved mother facing the destructiveness of the sea which has drowned the last of her six sons, Synge composed a dramatic dirge that universalizes the pathos of old age and the terror of death. By the use of concrete symbolic details and simple poetic dialogue, Synge evoked a mood of stoical acceptance that dignified the primitive humanity of the helpless survivors.

The slight narrative framework of the play is based on an actual incident observed by Synge in the Aran Islands. Watching the burial of a young man whose body had been washed up by the sea, Synge had a tragic premonition that all these fishermen and voyagers on the dangerous sea were doomed, sooner or later, to be "battered naked on the rocks." The inevitable triumph of the remorseless sea, he felt, intensified the natural anguish of the Aran women. "The maternal feeling is so strong in these islands that it gives a life of torment to the women." In his depiction of old Maurya's grief— "all passion spent"—rendered in speeches of great lyric beauty, Synge created a figure of stark, epic dignity.

CHARACTERS

MAURYA (an old woman)   BARTLEY (her son)
CATHLEEN (her daugh-   NORA (a younger
   ter)   daughter)
MEN and WOMEN

SCENE. *An Island Off the West of Ireland.*

(*Cottage kitchen, with nets, oil-skins, spinning-wheel, some new boards standing by the wall, etc.* CATHLEEN, *a girl of about twenty, finishes kneading cake, and puts it down in the pot-oven by the fire; then wipes her hands, and begins to spin at the wheel.* NORA, *a young girl, puts her head in at the door.*)

NORA (*in a low voice*). Where is she?

CATHLEEN. She's lying down, God help her, and may be sleeping, if she's able.

(NORA *comes in softly, and takes a bundle from under her shawl.*)

(*Spinning the wheel rapidly.*) What is it you have?

NORA. The young priest is after bringing them. It's a shirt and a plain stocking were got off a drowned man in Donegal.

(CATHLEEN *stops her wheel with a sudden movement, and leans out to listen.*)

We're to find out if it's Michael's they are, some time herself will be down looking by the sea.

CATHLEEN. How would they be Michael's, Nora. How would he go the length of that way to the far north?

NORA. The young priest says he's known the like of it. "If it's Michael's they are," says he, "you can tell herself he's got a clean burial by the grace of God, and if they're not his, let no one say a word about them, for she'll be getting her death," says he, "with crying and lamenting."

(*The door which* NORA *half closed is blown open by a gust of wind.*)

CATHLEEN (*looking out anxiously*). Did you ask him

88

would he stop Bartley going this day with the horses to the Galway fair?

NORA. "I won't stop him," says he, "but let you not be afraid. Herself does be saying prayers half through the night, and the Almighty God won't leave her destitute," says he, "with no son living."

CATHLEEN. Is the sea bad by the white rocks, Nora?

NORA. Middling bad, God help us. There's a great roaring in the west, and it's worse it'll be getting when the tide's turned to the wind. (*She goes over to the table with the bundle.*) Shall I open it now?

CATHLEEN. Maybe she'd wake up on us, and come in before we'd done. (*Coming to the table.*) It's a long time we'll be, and the two of us crying.

NORA (*goes to the inner door and listens*). She's moving about on the bed. She'll be coming in a minute.

CATHLEEN. Give me the ladder, and I'll put them up in the turf-loft, the way she won't know of them at all, and maybe when the tide turns she'll be going down to see would he be floating from the east.

(*They put the ladder against the gable of the chimney;* CATHLEEN *goes up a few steps and hides the bundle in the turf-loft.* MAURYA *comes from the inner room.*)

MAURYA (*looking up at* CATHLEEN *and speaking querulously*). Isn't it turf enough you have for this day and evening?

CATHLEEN. There's a cake baking at the fire for a short space (*Throwing down the turf.*) and Bartley will want it when the tide turns if he goes to Connemara.

(NORA *picks up the turf and puts it round the pot-oven.*)

MAURYA (*sitting down on a stool at the fire.*) He won't go this day with the wind rising from the south and west. He won't go this day, for the young priest will stop him surely.

NORA. He'll not stop him, mother, and I heard Eamon Simon and Stephen Pheety and Colum Shawn saying he would go.

MAURYA. Where is he itself?

NORA. He went down to see would there be another boat sailing in the week, and I'm thinking it won't be long till he's here now, for the tide's turning at the green head, and the hooker's tacking from the east.

CATHLEEN. I hear someone passing the big stones.

NORA (*looking out*). He's coming now, and he in a hurry.

BARTLEY (*comes in and looks round the room. Speaking sadly and quietly*). Where is the bit of new rope, Cathleen, was bought in Connemara?

CATHLEEN (*coming down*). Give it to him, Nora; it's on a nail by the white boards. I hung it up this morning, for the pig with the black feet was eating it.

NORA (*giving him a rope*). Is that it, Bartley?

MAURYA. You'd do right to leave that rope, Bartley, hanging by the boards. (BARTLEY *takes the rope.*) It will be wanting in this place, I'm telling you, if Michael is washed up tomorrow morning, or the next morning, or any morning in the week, for it's a deep grave we'll make him by the grace of God.

BARTLEY (*beginning to work with the rope*). I've no halter the way I can ride down on the mare, and I must go now quickly. This is the one boat going for two weeks or beyond it, and the fair will be a good fair for horses I heard them saying below.

MAURYA. It's a hard thing they'll be saying below if the body is washed up and there's no man in it to make the coffin, and I after giving a big price for the finest white boards you'd find in Connemara. (*She looks round at the boards.*)

BARTLEY. How would it be washed up, and we after looking each day for nine days, and a strong wind blowing a while back from the west and south?

MAURYA. If it wasn't found itself, that wind is raising the sea, and there was a star up against the moon, and it rising in the night. If it was a hundred horses, or a thousand horses you had itself, what is the price of a thousand horses against a son where there is one son only?

BARTLEY (*working at the halter, to* CATHLEEN). Let you go down each day, and see the sheep aren't jumping in on the rye, and if the jobber comes you can sell the pig with the black feet if there is a good price going.

MAURYA. How would the like of her get a good price for a pig?

BARTLEY (*to* CATHLEEN). If the west wind holds with the last bit of the moon let you and Nora get up weed enough for another cock for the kelp. It's hard set we'll be from this day with no one in it but one man to work.

MAURYA. It's hard set we'll be surely the day you're drown'd with the rest. What way will I live and the girls with me, and I an old woman looking for the grave?

(BARTLEY *lays down the halter, takes off his old coat, and puts on a newer one of the same flannel.*)

BARTLEY (*to* NORA). Is she coming to the pier?

NORA (*looking out*). She's passing the green head and letting fall her sails.

BARTLEY (*getting his purse and tobacco*). I'll have half an hour to go down, and you'll see me coming again in two days, or in three days, or maybe in four days if the wind is bad.

MAURYA (*turning round to the fire, and putting her shawl over her head*). Isn't it a hard and cruel man won't hear a word from an old woman, and she holding him from the sea?

CATHLEEN. It's the life of a young man to be going on the sea, and who would listen to an old woman with one thing and she saying it over?

BARTLEY (*taking the halter*). I must go now quickly. I'll ride down on the red mare, and the grey pony'll run behind me. . . . The blessing of God on you. (*He goes out.*)

MAURYA (*crying out as he is in the door*). He's gone now, God spare us, and we'll not see him again. He's gone now, and when the black night is falling I'll have no son left me in the world.

CATHLEEN. Why wouldn't you give him your blessing and he looking round in the door? Isn't it sorrow enough

is on every one in this house without your sending him
out with an unlucky word behind him, and a hard word
in his ear?

(MAURYA *takes up the tongs and begins raking the fire
aimlessly without looking round.*)

NORA (*turning towards her*). You're taking away the
turf from the cake.

CATHLEEN (*crying out*). The Son of God forgive us,
Nora, we're after forgetting his bit of bread. (*She comes
over to the fire.*)

NORA. And it's destroyed he'll be going till dark night,
and he after eating nothing since the sun went up.

CATHLEEN (*turning the cake out of the oven*). It's destroyed he'll be, surely. There's no sense left on any person in a house where an old woman will be talking for
ever.

(MAURYA *sways herself on her stool.*)
(*Cutting off some of the bread and rolling it in a cloth;
to* MAURYA.) Let you go down now to the spring well and
give him this and he passing. You'll see him then and the
dark word will be broken, and you can say "God speed
you," the way he'll be easy in his mind.

MAURYA (*taking the bread*). Will I be in it as soon as
himself?

CATHLEEN. If you go now quickly.

MAURYA (*standing up unsteadily*). It's hard set I am
to walk.

CATHLEEN (*looking at her anxiously*). Give her the
stick, Nora, or maybe she'll slip on the big stones.

NORA. What stick?

CATHLEEN. The stick Michael brought from Connemara.

MAURYA (*taking a stick* NORA *gives her*). In the big
world the old people do be leaving things after them for
their sons and children, but in this place it is the young
men do be leaving things behind for them that do be old.
(*She goes out slowly.* NORA *goes over to the ladder.*)

CATHLEEN. Wait, Nora, maybe she'd turn back quickly.

She's that sorry, God help her, you wouldn't know the thing she'd do.

NORA. Is she gone round by the bush?

CATHLEEN (*looking out*). She's gone now. Throw it down quickly, for the Lord knows when she'll be out of it again.

NORA (*getting the bundle from the loft*). The young priest said he'd be passing tomorrow, and we might go down and speak to him below if it's Michael's they are surely.

CATHLEEN (*taking the bundle*). Did he say what way they were found?

NORA (*coming down*). "There were two men," says he, "and they rowing round with poteen before the cocks crowed, and the oar of one of them caught the body, and they passing the black cliffs of the north."

CATHLEEN (*trying to open the bundle*). Give me a knife, Nora, the string's perished with the salt water, and there's a black knot on it you wouldn't loosen in a week.

NORA (*giving her a knife*). I've heard tell it was a long way to Donegal.

CATHLEEN (*cutting the string*). It is surely. There was a man in here a while ago—the man sold us that knife— and he said if you set off walking from the rocks beyond, it would be seven days you'd be in Donegal.

NORA. And what time would a man take, and he floating?

(CATHLEEN *opens the bundle and takes out a bit of a stocking. They look at them eagerly.*)

CATHLEEN (*in a low voice*). The Lord spare us, Nora! isn't it a queer hard thing to say if it's his they are surely?

NORA. I'll get his shirt off the hook the way we can put the one flannel on the other. (*She looks through some clothes hanging in the corner.*) It's not with them, Cathleen, and where will it be?

CATHLEEN. I'm thinking Bartley put it on him in the morning, for his own shirt was heavy with the salt in it. (*Pointing to the corner.*) There's a bit of a sleeve was of the same stuff. Give me that and it will do.

(NORA *brings it to her and they compare the flannel*.) It's the same stuff, Nora; but if it is itself aren't there great rolls of it in the shops of Galway, and isn't it many another man may have a shirt of it as well as Michael himself?

NORA (*who has taken up the stockings and counted the stitches, crying out*). It's Michael, Cathleen, it's Michael; God spare his soul, and what will herself say when she hears this story, and Bartley on the sea?

CATHLEEN (*taking the stocking*). It's a plain stocking.

NORA. It's the second one of the third pair I knitted, and I put up three score stitches, and I dropped four of them.

CATHLEEN (*counts the stitches*). It's that number is in it. (*Crying out*.) Ah, Nora, isn't it a bitter thing to think of him floating that way to the far north, and no one to keen him but the black hags that do be flying on the sea?

NORA (*swinging herself round, and throwing out her arms on the clothes*). And isn't it a pitiful thing when there is nothing left of a man who was a great rower and fisher, but a bit of an old shirt and a plain stocking?

CATHLEEN (*after an instant*). Tell me is herself coming, Nora? I hear a little sound on the path.

NORA (*looking out*). She is, Cathleen. She's coming up to the door.

CATHLEEN. Put these things away before she'll come in. Maybe it's easier she'll be after giving her blessing to Bartley, and we won't let on we've heard anything the time he's on the sea.

NORA (*helping* CATHLEEN *to close the bundle*). We'll put them here in the corner.

(*They put them into a hole in the chimney corner.* CATHLEEN *goes back to the spinning-wheel.*)
Will she see it was crying I was?

CATHLEEN. Keep your back to the door the way the light'll not be on you.

(NORA *sits down at the chimney corner, with her back to the door.* MAURYA *comes in very slowly, without looking at the girls, and goes over to her stool at the other side of the fire. The cloth with the bread is still in her hand. The girls look at each other, and* NORA *points to the bundle of bread.*)

(*After spinning for a moment.*) You didn't give him his bit of bread?

(MAURYA *begins to keen softly, without turning round.*) Did you see him riding down?

(MAURYA *goes on keening.*)

(*A little impatiently.*) God forgive you; isn't it a better thing to raise your voice and tell what you seen, than to be making lamentation for a thing that's done? Did you see Bartley, I'm saying to you.

MAURYA (*with a weak voice*). My heart's broken from this day.

CATHLEEN (*as before*). Did you see Bartley?

MAURYA. I seen the fearfulest thing.

CATHLEEN (*leaves her wheel and looks out*). God forgive you; he's riding the mare now over the green head, and the grey pony behind him.

MAURYA (*starts, so that her shawl falls back from her head and shows her white tossed hair. With a frightened voice*). The grey pony behind him.

CATHLEEN (*coming to the fire*). What is it ails you, at all?

MAURYA (*speaking very slowly*). I've seen the fearfulest thing any person has seen, since the day Bride Dara seen the dead man with the child in his arms.

CATHLEEN *and* NORA. Uah. (*They crouch down in front of the old woman at the fire.*)

NORA. Tell us what it is you seen.

MAURYA. I went down to the spring well, and I stood there saying a prayer to myself. Then Bartley came along, and he riding on the red mare with the grey pony behind him. (*She puts up her hands, as if to hide something from her eyes.*) The Son of God spare us, Nora!

CATHLEEN. What is it you seen?

MAURYA. I seen Michael himself.

CATHLEEN (*speaking softly*). You did not, mother; it wasn't Michael you seen, for his body is after being found in the far north, and he's got a clean burial by the grace of God.

MAURYA (*a little defiantly*). I'm after seeing him this day, and he riding and galloping. Bartley came first on the red mare; and I tried to say "God speed you," but something choked the words in my throat. He went by quickly; and "the blessing of God on you," says he, and I could say nothing. I looked up then, and I crying, at the grey pony, and there was Michael upon it—with fine clothes on him, and new shoes on his feet.

CATHLEEN (*begins to keen*). It's destroyed we are from this day. It's destroyed, surely.

NORA. Didn't the young priest say the Almighty God wouldn't leave her destitute with no son living?

MAURYA (*in a low voice, but clearly*). It's little the like of him knows of the sea. . . . Bartley will be lost now, and let you call in Eamon and make me a good coffin out of the white boards, for I won't live after them. I've had a husband, and a husband's father, and six sons in this house—six fine men, though it was a hard birth I had with every one of them and they coming to the world—and some of them were found and some of them were not found, but they're gone now the lot of them. . . . There were Stephen, and Shawn, were lost in the great wind, and found after in the Bay of Gregory of the Golden Mouth, and carried up the two of them on the one plank, and in by that door. (*She pauses for a moment, the girls start as if they heard something through the door that is half open behind them.*)

NORA (*in a whisper*). Did you hear that, Cathleen? Did you hear a noise in the north-east?

CATHLEEN (*in a whisper*). There's someone after crying out by the seashore.

MAURYA (*continues without hearing anything*). There was Sheamus and his father, and his own father again, were lost in a dark night, and not a stick or sign was seen of them when the sun went up. There was Patch after was drowned out of a curragh that turned over. I was sitting here with Bartley, and he a baby, lying on my two knees, and I seen two women, and three women, and four women coming in, and they crossing themselves, and not saying a word. I looked out then, and there were men coming after them, and they holding a thing in the half of a red sail, and water dripping out of it—it was a dry day, Nora— and leaving a track to the door. (*She pauses again with her hand stretched out towards the door. It opens softly and old women begin to come in, crossing themselves on the threshold, and kneeling down in front of the stage with red petticoats over their heads.*)

(*Half in a dream, to* CATHLEEN.) Is it Patch, or Michael, or what is it at all?

CATHLEEN. Michael is after being found in the far north, and when he is found there how could he be here in this place?

MAURYA. There does be a power of young men floating round in the sea, and what way would they know if it was Michael they had, or another man like him, for when a man is nine days in the sea, and the wind blowing, it's hard set his own mother would be to say what man was it.

CATHLEEN. It's Michael, God spare him, for they're after sending us a bit of his clothes from the far north. (*She reaches out and hands* MAURYA *the clothes that belonged to* MICHAEL. MAURYA *stands up slowly and takes them in her hands.* NORA *looks out.*)

NORA. They're carrying a thing among them and there's water dripping out of it and leaving a track by the big stones.

CATHLEEN (*in a whisper to the women who have come in*). Is it Bartley it is?

ONE OF THE WOMEN. It is surely, God rest his soul.

(*Two younger women come in and pull out the table. Then men carry in the body of* BARTLEY, *laid on a plank, with a bit of a sail over it, and lay it on the table.*)

CATHLEEN (*to the women, as they are doing so*). What way was he drowned?

ONE OF THE WOMEN. The grey pony knocked him into the sea, and he was washed out where there is a great surf on the white rocks.

(MAURYA *has gone over and knelt down at the head of the table. The women are keening softly and swaying themselves with a slow movement.* CATHLEEN *and* NORA *kneel at the other end of the table. The men kneel near the door.*)

MAURYA (*raising her head and speaking as if she did not see the people around her*). They're all gone now, and there isn't anything more the sea can do to me. . . . I'll have no call now to be up crying and praying when the wind breaks from the south, and you can hear the surf is in the east, and the surf is in the west, making a great stir with the two noises, and they hitting one on the other. I'll have no call now to be going down and getting Holy Water in the dark nights after Samhain, and I won't care what way the sea is when the other women will be keening. (*To* NORA.) Give me the Holy Water, Nora, there's a small sup still on the dresser.

(NORA *gives it to her.*)

(*Drops* MICHAEL'S *clothes across* BARTLEY'S *feet, and sprinkles the Holy Water over him.*) It isn't that I haven't prayed for you, Bartley, to the Almighty God. It isn't that I haven't said prayers in the dark night till you wouldn't know what I'd be saying; but it's a great rest I'll have now, and it's time surely. It's a great rest I'll have now, and great sleeping in the long nights after Samhain, if it's only a bit of wet flour we do have to eat, and maybe a fish that would be stinking. (*She kneels down again, crossing herself, and saying prayers under her breath.*)

CATHLEEN (*to an old man*). Maybe yourself and Eamon would make a coffin when the sun rises. We have fine white boards herself bought, God help her, thinking Michael would be found, and I have a new cake you can eat while you'll be working.

THE OLD MAN (*looking at the boards*). Are there nails with them?

CATHLEEN. There are not, Colum; we didn't think of the nails.

ANOTHER MAN. It's a great wonder she wouldn't think

of the nails, and all the coffins she's seen made already.

CATHLEEN. It's getting old she is, and broken.

(MAURYA *stands up again very slowly and spreads out the pieces of* MICHAEL's *clothes beside the body, sprinkling them with the last of the Holy Water.*)

NORA (*in a whisper to* CATHLEEN). She's quiet now and easy; but the day Michael was drowned you could hear her crying out from this to the spring well. It's fonder she was of Michael, and would any one have thought that?

CATHLEEN (*slowly and clearly*). An old woman will be soon tired with anything she will do, and isn't it nine days herself is after crying and keening, and making great sorrow in the house?

MAURYA (*puts the empty cup mouth downwards on the table, and lays her hands together on* BARTLEY's *feet*). They're all together this time, and the end is come. May the Almighty God have mercy on Bartley's soul, and on Michael's soul, and on the souls of Sheamus and Patch, and Stephen and Shawn (*Bending her head.*); and may He have mercy on my soul, Nora, and on the soul of every one is left living in the world. (*She pauses, and the keen rises a little more loudly from the women, then sinks away.*)

(*Continuing.*) Michael has a clean burial in the far north, by the grace of the Almighty God. Bartley will have a fine coffin out of the white boards, and a deep grave surely. What more can we want than that? No man at all can be living for ever, and we must be satisfied. (*She kneels down again and the curtain falls slowly.*)

ILE

by Eugene O'Neill

EUGENE O'NEILL's passionate interest in the sea, ships, and sailors remained with him all his life and influenced both his philosophy and his creative career. An omnivorous reader in his youth, he particularly enjoyed the romantic tales of Jack London, Kipling, and Conrad. In the early 1900's when his family lived in New London, he enjoyed watching the arrival and departure of the beautiful square-riggers in the harbor. In 1910, after a quarrel with his father, he signed on as a seaman aboard a Norwegian three-master ship sailing for Buenos Aires. On this sixty-five-day voyage he gained first-hand knowledge of the seaman's life and character. Later he journeyed as a seaman to South Africa and England. Like Herman Melville, O'Neill believed his real education came not from schools but from the sea and sailors. His first produced play was the one act *Bound East for Cardiff*. Time and again in his long and distinguished dramatic career he returned to the theme of the relationship of man to the sea.

Mary Heaton Vorse, a Provincetown writer, suggested the plot of *Ile* to O'Neill. She had known a Captain John Cook, who in 1903 had driven his men to mutiny and caused the insanity of his wife by his stubborn insistence on getting his quota of oil after a two-year voyage. Several years after he had written the play, O'Neill met the poor deranged wife in Provincetown.

CHARACTERS

BEN (the cabin boy)

THE STEWARD

CAPTAIN KEENEY

SLOCUM (second mate)

MRS. KEENEY

JOE (a harpooner)

MEMBERS OF THE CREW of the steam whaler *Atlantic Queen*

SCENE CAPTAIN KEENEY's *cabin on board the steam whaling ship* Atlantic Queen—*a small, square compartment about eight feet high with a skylight in the center looking out on the poop deck. On the left [the stern of the ship] a long bench with rough cushions is built in against the wall. In front of the bench, a table. Over the bench, several curtained portholes.*

In the rear, left, a door leading to the CAPTAIN's *sleeping quarters. To the right of the door a small organ, looking as if it were brand new, is placed against the wall.*

On the right, to the rear, a marble-topped sideboard. On the sideboard, a woman's sewing basket. Farther forward, a doorway leading to the companion way, and past the officer's quarters to the main deck.

In the center of the room, a stove. From the middle of the ceiling a hanging lamp is suspended. The walls of the cabin are painted white.

There is no rolling of the ship, and the light which comes through the skylight is sickly and faint, indicating one of those gray days of calm when ocean and sky are alike dead. The silence is unbroken except for the measured tread of some one walking up and down on the poop deck overhead.

It is nearing two bells—one o'clock—in the afternoon of a day in the year 1895.

At the rise of the curtain there is a moment of intense silence. Then the STEWARD *enters and commences to clear the table of the few dishes which still remain on it after the* CAPTAIN's *dinner. He is an old, grizzled man dressed in dungaree pants, a sweater,*

104

*and a woolen cap with ear flaps. His manner is sullen
and angry. He stops stacking up the plates and casts a
quick glance upward at the skylight; then tiptoes
over to the closed door in rear and listens with his
ear pressed to the crack. What he hears makes his
face darken and he mutters a furious curse. There is
a noise from the doorway on the right and he darts
back to the table.*

    BEN *enters. He is an overgrown, gawky boy with a
long, pinched face. He is dressed in sweater, fur cap,
etc. His teeth are chattering with the cold and he
hurries to the stove, where he stands for a moment
shivering, blowing on his hands, slapping them
against his sides, on the verge of crying.*

THE STEWARD [*In relieved tones—seeing who it is.*]
Oh, 'tis you, is it? What're ye shiverin' 'bout? Stay by the
stove where ye belong and ye'll find no need of chatterin'.

    BEN   It's c-c-cold. [*Trying to control his chattering
teeth—derisively.*] Who d'ye think it were—the Old
Man?

THE STEWARD—[*Makes a threatening move*—BEN
shrinks away.]   None o' your lip, young un, or I'll learn
ye. [*More kindly.*] Where was it ye've been all o' the time
—the fo'c'stle?

    BEN   Yes.

THE STEWARD   Let the Old Man see ye up for'ard mon-
keyshinin' with the hands and ye'll get a hidin' ye'll not
forget in a hurry.

    BEN   Aw, he don't see nothin'. [*A trace of awe in his
tones—he glances upward.*] He just walks up and down
like he didn't notice nobody—and stares at the ice to the
no'th'ard.

THE STEWARD [*The same tone of awe creeping into his
voice.*]   He's always starin' at the ice. [*In a sudden rage,
shaking his fist at the skylight.*] Ice, ice, ice! Damn him
and damn the ice! Holdin' us in for nigh on a year—nothin' to see but ice—stuck in it like a fly in molasses!

    BEN [*Apprehensively.*]   Ssshh! He'll hear ye.

THE STEWARD [*Raging.*]   Aye, damn him, and damn
the Arctic seas, and damn this stinkin' whalin' ship of his,
and damn me for a fool to ever ship on it! [*Subsiding as
if realizing the uselessness of this outburst—shaking his
head—slowly, with deep conviction.*] He's a hard man—
as hard a man as ever sailed the seas.

BEN [*Solemnly.*]   Aye.

THE STEWARD   The two years we all signed up for are
done this day. Blessed Christ! Two years o' this dog's life,
and no luck in the fishin', and the hands half starved with
the food runnin' low, rotten as it is; and not a sign of him
turnin' back for home! [*Bitterly.*] Home! I begin to doubt
if ever I'll set foot on land again. [*Excitedly.*] What is it
he thinks he' goin' to do? Keep us all up here after our
time is worked out till the last man of us is starved to
death or frozen? We've grub enough hardly to last out
the voyage back if we started now. What are the men goin'
to do 'bout it? Did ye hear any talk in the fo'c'stle?

BEN [*Going over to him—in a half whisper.*]   They
said if he don't put back south for home to-day they're
goin' to mutiny.

THE STEWARD [*With grim satisfaction.*]   Mutiny? Aye,
'tis the only thing they can do; and serve him right after
the manner he's treated them—'s if they wern't no better
nor dogs.

BEN   The ice is all broke up to s'uth'ard. They's clear
water 's far 's you can see. He ain't got no excuse for not
turnin' back for home, the men says.

THE STEWARD [*Bitterly.*]   He won't look nowheres but
no'th'ard where they's only the ice to see. He don't want
to see no clear water. All he thinks on is gittin' the ile—'s
if it was our fault he ain't had good luck with the whales.
[*Shaking his head.*] I think the man's mighty nigh losin'
his senses.

BEN [*Awed.*]   D'you really think he's crazy?

THE STEWARD   Aye, it's the punishment o' God on him.
Did ye ever hear of a man who wasn't crazy do the things
he does? [*Pointing to the door in rear.*] Who but a man
that's mad would take his woman—and as sweet a woman

as ever was—on a stinkin' whalin' ship to the Arctic seas
to be locked in by the rotten ice for nigh on a year, and
maybe lose her senses forever—for it's sure she'll never
be the same again.

BEN [*Sadly.*]   She useter be awful nice to me before—— [*His eyes grow wide and frightened.*] she got—
like she is.

THE STEWARD   Aye, she was good to all of us. 'Twould
have been hell on board without her, for he's a hard man
—a hard, hard man—a driver if there ever was one. [*With
a grim laugh.*] I hope he's satisfied now—drivin' her on till
she's near lost her mind. And who could blame her? 'Tis
a God's wonder we're not a ship full of crazed people—
with the damned ice all the time, and the quiet so thick
you're afraid to hear your own voice.

BEN [*With a frightened glance toward the door on
right.*]   She don't never speak to me no more—jest looks
at me 's if she didn't know me.

THE STEWARD   She don't know no one—but him. She
talks to him—when she does talk—right enough.

BEN   She does nothin' all day long now but sit and sew
—and then she cries to herself without makin' no noise.
I've seen her.

THE STEWARD   Aye, I could hear her through the door
a while back.

BEN [*Tiptoes over to the door and listens.*]   She's
cryin' now.

THE STEWARD [*Furiously—shaking his fist.*]   God send
his soul to hell for the devil he is!

[*There is the noise of someone coming slowly down
the companionway stairs.* THE STEWARD *hurries to his
stacked up dishes. He is so nervous from fright that
he knocks off the top one, which falls and breaks on
the floor. He stands aghast, trembling with dread.* BEN
*is violently rubbing off the organ with a piece of cloth
which he has snatched from his pocket.* CAPTAIN
KEENEY *appears in the doorway on right and comes
into the cabin, removing his fur cap as he does so. He*

is a man of about forty, around five-ten in height but looking much shorter on account of the enormous proportions of his shoulders and chest. His face is massive and deeply lined, with gray-blue eyes of a bleak hardness, and a tightly clenched, thin-lipped mouth. His thick hair is long and gray. He is dressed in a heavy blue jacket and blue pants stuffed into his sea-boots.

[He is followed into the cabin by the SECOND MATE, *a rangy six-footer with a lean weather-beaten face. The* MATE *is dressed about the same as the captain. He is a man of thirty or so.]*

KEENEY [*Comes toward the* STEWARD—*with a stern look on his face. The* STEWARD *is visibly frightened and the stack of dishes rattles in his trembling hands.* KEENEY *draws back his fist and the* STEWARD *shrinks away. The fist is gradually lowered and* KEENEY *speaks slowly.*] 'Twould be like hitting a worm. It is nigh on two bells, Mr. Steward, and this truck not cleared yet.

THE STEWARD [*Stammering.*]   Y-y-yes, sir.

KEENEY   Instead of doin' your rightful work ye've been below here gossipin' old woman's talk with that boy. [*To* BEN, *fiercely.*] Get out o' this, you! Clean up the chart room. [BEN *darts past the* MATE *to the open doorway.*] Pick up that dish, Mr. Steward!

THE STEWARD [*Doing so with difficulty.*]   Yes, sir.

KEENEY   The next dish you break, Mr. Steward, you take a bath in the Bering Sea at the end of a rope.

THE STEWARD [*Trembling.*]   Yes, sir. [*He hurries out. The* SECOND MATE *walks slowly over to the* CAPTAIN.]

MATE   I warn't 'specially anxious the man at the wheel should catch what I wanted to say to you, sir. That's why I asked you to come below.

KEENEY [*Impatiently.*]   Speak your say, Mr. Slocum.

MATE [*Unconsciously lowering his voice.*]   I'm afeard there'll be trouble with the hands by the look o' things. They'll likely turn ugly, every blessed one o' them, if you don't put back. The two years they signed up for is up to-day.

KEENEY   And d'you think you're tellin' me somethin' new, Mr. Slocum? I've felt it in the air this long time past. D'you think I've not seen their ugly looks and the grudgin' way they worked?

[*The door in rear is opened and* MRS. KEENEY *stands in the doorway. She is a slight, sweet-faced little woman primly dressed in black. Her eyes are red from weeping and her face drawn and pale. She takes in the cabin with a frightened glance and stands as if fixed to the spot by some nameless dread, clasping and unclasping her hands nervously. The two men turn and look at her.*]

[*With rough tenderness.*] Well, Annie?

MRS. KEENEY [*As if awakening from a dream.*]   David, I—— [*She is silent. The* MATE *starts for the doorway.*]

KEENEY [*Turning to him—sharply.*]   Wait!

MATE   Yes, sir.

KEENEY   D'you want anything, Annie?

MRS. KEENEY [*After a pause, during which she seems to be endeavoring to collect her thoughts.*]   I thought maybe—I'd go up on deck, David, to get a breath of fresh air. [*She stands humbly awaiting his permission. He and the* MATE *exchange a significant glance.*]

KEENEY   It's too cold, Annie. You'd best stay below to-day. There's nothing to look at on deck—but ice.

MRS. KEENEY [*Monotonously.*]   I know—ice, ice, ice. But there's nothing to see down here but these walls. [*She makes a gesture of loathing.*]

KEENEY   You can play the organ, Annie.

MRS. KEENEY [*Dully.*]   I hate the organ. It puts me in mind of home.

KEENEY [*A touch of resentment in his voice.*]   I got it jest for you.

MRS. KEENEY [*Dully.*]   I know. [*She turns away from them and walks slowly to the bench on left. She lifts up*

*one of the curtains and looks through the porthole; then
utters an exclamation of joy.*] Ah, water! Clear water!
As far as I can see! How good it looks after all these
months of ice! [*She turns round to them, her face trans-
figured with joy.*] Ah, now I must go up on deck and look
at it, David.

KEENEY [*Frowning.*]   Best not to-day, Annie. Best
wait for a day when the sun shines.

MRS. KEENEY [*Desperately.*]   But the sun never shines
in this terrible place.

KEENEY [*A tone of command in his voice.*]   Best not
to-day, Annie.

MRS. KEENEY [*Crumbling before this command—ab-
jectly.*]   Very well, David. [*She stands there staring
straight before her as if in a daze. The two men look at
her uneasily.*]

KEENEY [*Sharply.*]   Annie!

MRS. KEENEY [*Dully.*]   Yes, David.

KEENEY   Me and Mr. Slocum has business to talk
about—ship's business.

MRS. KEENEY   Very well, David. [*She goes slowly out,
rear, and leaves the door three-quarters shut behind her.*]

KEENEY   Best not have her on deck if they's goin' to
be any trouble.

MATE   Yes, sir.

KEENEY   And trouble they's goin' to be. I feel it in my
bones. [*Takes a revolver from the pocket of his coat and
examines it.*] Got your'n?

MATE   Yes, sir.

KEENEY   Not that we'll have to use 'em—not if I know
their breed of dog—jest to frighten 'em up a bit. [*Grimly.*]
I ain't never been forced to use one yit; and trouble I've
had by land and by sea 's long as I kin remember, and
will have till my dyin' day, I reckon.

MATE [*Hesitatingly.*]   Then you ain't goin'—to turn
back?

KEENEY   Turn back! Mr. Slocum, did you ever hear
'o me pointin' s'uth for home with only a measly four hundred barrel of ile in the hold?

MATE [*Hastily.*] No, sir—but the grub's gittin' low.

KEENEY They's enough to last a long time yit, if they're careful with it; and they's plenty o' water.

MATE They say it's not fit to eat—what's left; and the two years they signed on fur is up to-day. They might make trouble for you in the courts when we git home.

KEENEY To hell with 'em! Let them make what law trouble they kin. I don't give a damn 'bout the money. I've got to git the ile! [*Glancing sharply at the* MATE.] You ain't turnin' no damned sea lawyer, be you, Mr. Slocum?

MATE [*Flushing.*] Not by a hell of a sight, sir.

KEENEY What do the fools want to go home fur now? Their share o' the four hundred barrel wouldn't keep 'em in chewin' terbacco.

MATE [*Slowly.*] They wants to git back to their folks an' things, I s'pose.

KEENEY [*Looking at him searchingly.*] 'N' you want to turn back, too. [*The* MATE *looks down confusedly before his sharp gaze.*] Don't lie, Mr. Slocum. It's writ down plain in your eyes. [*With grim sarcasm.*] I hope, Mr. Slocum, you ain't agoin' to jine the men agin me.

MATE [*Indignantly.*] That ain't fair, sir, to say sich things.

KEENEY [*With satisfaction.*] I warn't much afeared o' that, Tom. You been with me nigh on ten year and I've learned ye whalin'. No man kin say I ain't a good master, if I be a hard one.

MATE I warn't thinkin' of myself, sir—'bout turnin' home, I mean. [*Desperately.*] But Mrs. Keeney, sir—seems like she ain't jest satisfied up here, ailin' like—what with the cold an' bad luck an' the ice an' all.

KEENEY [*His face clouding—rebukingly but not severely.*] That's my business, Mr. Slocum. I'll thank you to steer a clear course o' that. [*A pause.*] The ice'll break up soon to no'th'ard. I could see it startin' to-day. And when it goes and we git some sun Annie'll perk up. [*Another pause—then he bursts forth.*] It ain't the damned money what's keepin' me up in the Northern seas, Tom.

But I can't go back to Homeport with a measly four hundred barrel of ile. I'd die fust. I ain't never came back home in all my days without a full ship. Ain't that truth?

MATE   Yes, sir; but this voyage you been icebound, an'——

KEENEY [*Scornfully.*]   And d'you s'pose any of 'em would believe that—any o' them skippers I've beaten voyage after voyage? Can't you hear 'em laughin' and sneerin'—Tibbots 'n' Harris 'n' Simms and the rest—and all o' Homeport makin' fun o' me? "Dave Keeney what boasts he's the best whalin' skipper out o' Homeport comin' back with a measly four hundred barrel of ile?" [*The thought of this drives him into a frenzy, and he smashes his fist down on the marble top of the sideboard.*] Hell! I got to git the ile, I tell you. How could I figger on this ice? It's never been so bad before in the thirty year I been acomin' here. And now it's breakin' up. In a couple o' days it'll be all gone. And they's whale here, plenty of 'em. I know they is and I ain't never gone wrong yit. I got to git the ile! I got to git it in spite of all hell, and by God, I ain't agoin' home till I do git it! [*There is the sound of subdued sobbing from the door in rear. The two men stand silent for a moment, listening. Then* KEENEY *goes over to the door and looks in. He hesitates for a moment as if he were going to enter—then closes the door softly.* JOE, *the harpooner, an enormous six-footer with a battered, ugly face, enters from right and stands waiting for the* CAPTAIN *to notice him.*]

[*Turning and seeing him.*] Don't be standin' there like a gawk, Harpooner. Speak up!

JOE [*Confusedly.*]   We want—the men, sir—they wants to send a depitation aft to have a word with you.

KEENEY [*Furiously.*]   Tell 'em to go to—— [*Checks himself and continues grimly.*] Tell 'em to come. I'll see 'em.

JOE   Aye, aye, sir. [*He goes out.*]

KEENEY [*With a grim smile.*]   Here it comes, the trouble you spoke of, Mr. Slocum, and we'll make short shift of it. It's better to crush such things at the start than let them make headway.

MATE [*Worriedly.*] Shall I wake up the First and Fourth, sir? We might need their help.

KEENEY No, let them sleep. I'm well able to handle this alone, Mr. Slocum. [*There is the shuffling of footsteps from outside and five of the crew crowd into the cabin, led by* JOE. *All are dressed alike—sweaters, seaboots, etc. They glance uneasily at the* CAPTAIN, *twirling their fur caps in their hands.*]

[*After a pause.*] Well? Who's to speak fur ye?

JOE [*Stepping forward with an air of bravado.*] I be.

KEENEY [*Eyeing him up and down coldly.*] So you be. Then speak your say and be quick about it.

JOE [*Trying not to wilt before the* CAPTAIN's *glance and avoiding his eyes.*] The time we signed up for is done to-day.

KEENEY [*Icily.*] You're tellin' me nothin' I don't know.

JOE You ain't pintin' fur home yit, far 's we kin see.

KEENEY No, and I ain't agoin' to till this ship is full of ile.

JOE You can't go no further no'th with the ice afore ye.

KEENEY The ice is breaking up.

JOE [*After a slight pause during which the others mumble angrily to one another.*] The grub we're gittin' now is rotten.

KEENEY It's good enough fur ye. Better men than ye have eaten worse. [*There is a chorus of angry exclamations from the crowd.*]

JOE [*Encouraged by this support.*] We ain't agoin' to work no more less you puts back for home.

KEENEY [*Fiercely.*] You ain't ain't you?

JOE No; and the law courts'll say we was right.

KEENEY To hell with your law courts! We're at sea now and I'm the law on this ship. [*Edging up toward the harpooner.*] And every mother's son of you what don't obey orders goes in irons. [*There are more angry exclamations from the crew.* MRS. KEENEY *appears in the door-*

way in rear and looks on with startled eyes. None of the men notice her.]

JOE [*With bravado.*]   Then we're agoin' to mutiny and take the old hooker home ourselves. Ain't we, boys? [*As he turns his head to look at the others,* KEENEY's *fist shoots out to the side of his jaw.* JOE *goes down in a heap and lies there.* MRS. KEENEY *gives a shriek and hides her face in her hands. The men pull out their sheath knives and start a rush, but stop when they find themselves confronted by the revolvers of* KEENEY *and the* MATE.]

KEENEY [*His eyes and voice snapping.*]   Hold still! [*The men stand huddled together in a sullen silence.* KEENEY's *voice is full of mockery.*]   You've found out it ain't safe to mutiny on this ship, ain't you? And now git for'ard where ye belong, and—— [*He gives* JOE's *body a contemptuous kick.*]   Drag him with you. And remember the first man of ye I see shirkin' I'll shoot dead as sure as there's a sea under us, and you can tell the rest the same. Git for'ard now! Quick! [*The men leave in cowed silence, carrying* JOE *with them.* KEENEY *turns to the* MATE *with a short laugh and puts his revolver back in his pocket.*]   Best get up on deck, Mr. Slocum, and see to it they don't try none of their skulkin' tricks. We'll have to keep an eye peeled from now on. I know 'em.

MATE   Yes, sir. [*He goes out, right.* KEENEY *hears his wife's hysterical weeping and turns around in surprise— then walks slowly to her side.*]

KEENEY [*Putting an arm around her shoulder—with gruff tenderness.*]   There, there, Annie. Don't be afeared. It's all past and gone.

MRS. KEENEY [*Shrinking away from him.*]   Oh, I can't bear it! I can't bear it any longer!

KEENEY [*Gently.*]   Can't bear what, Annie?

MRS. KEENEY [*Hysterically.*]   All this horrible brutality, and these brutes of men, and this terrible ship, and this prison cell of a room, and the ice all around, and the silence. [*After this outburst she calms down and wipes her eyes with her handkerchief.*]

KEENEY [*After a pause during which he looks down at*

her with a puzzled frown.]   Remember, I warn't hanker-in' to have you come on this voyage, Annie.

MRS. KEENEY   I wanted to be with you, David, don't you see? I didn't want to wait back there in the house all alone as I've been doing these last six years since we were married—waiting, and watching, and fearing—with noth-ing to keep my mind occupied—not able to go back teach-ing school on account of being Dave Keeney's wife. I used to dream of sailing on the great, wide, glorious ocean. I wanted to be by your side in the danger and vigorous life of it all. I wanted to see you the hero they make you out to be in Homeport. And instead—— [*Her voice grows tremulous.*] All I find is ice and cold—and brutality! [*Her voice breaks.*]

KEENEY   I warned you what it'd be, Annie. "Whalin' ain't no ladies' tea party," I says to you, and "you better stay to home where you've got all your woman's com-forts." [*Shaking his head.*] But you was so set on it.

MRS. KEENEY [*Wearily.*]   Oh, I know it isn't your fault, David. You see, I didn't believe you. I guess I was dreaming about the old Vikings in the story books and I thought you were one of them.

KEENEY [*Protestingly.*]   I done my best to make it as cozy and comfortable as could be. [MRS. KEENEY *looks around her in wild scorn.*] I even sent to the city for that organ for ye, thinkin' it might be soothin' to ye to be play-in' it times when they was calms and things was dull like.

MRS. KEENEY [*Wearily.*]   Yes, you were very kind, David. I know that. [*She goes to left and lifts the curtains from the porthole and looks out—then suddenly bursts forth.*] I won't stand it—I can't stand it—pent up by these walls like a prisoner. [*She runs over to him and throws her arms around him, weeping. He puts his arm protectingly over her shoulders.*] Take me away from here, David! If I don't get away from here, out of this ter-rible ship, I'll go mad! Take me home, David! I can't think any more. I feel as if the cold and the silence were crushing down on my brain. I'm afraid. Take me home!

KEENEY [*Holds her at arm's length and looks at her*

face anxiously.]   Best go to bed, Annie. You ain't your-self. You got fever. Your eyes look so strange like. I ain't never seen you look this way before.

MRS. KEENEY [*Laughing hysterically*.]   It's the ice and the cold and the silence—they'd make any one look strange.

KEENEY [*Soothingly*.]   In a month or two, with good luck, three at the most, I'll have her filled with ile and then we'll give her everything she'll stand and pint for home.

MRS. KEENEY   But we can't wait for that—I can't wait. I want to get home. And the men won't wait. They want to get home. It's cruel, it's brutal for you to keep them. You must sail back. You've got no excuse. There's clear water to the south now. If you've a heart at all you've got to turn back.

KEENEY [*Harshly*.]   I can't, Annie.

MRS. KEENEY   Why can't you?

KEENEY   A woman couldn't rightly understand my reason.

MRS. KEENEY [*Wildly*.]   Because it's a stupid, stub-born reason. Oh, I heard you talking with the second mate. You're afraid the other captains will sneer at you because you didn't come back with a full ship. You want to live up to your silly reputation and starve men and drive me mad to do it.

KEENEY [*His jaw set stubbornly*.]   It ain't that, Annie. Them skippers would never dare sneer to my face. It ain't so much what any one'd say—but—— [*He hesitates, struggling to express his meaning*.] You see—I've always done it—since my first voyage as skipper. I always come back—with a full ship—and—it don't seem right not to —somehow. I been always first whalin' skipper out o' Homeport, and—— Don't you see my meanin', Annie? [*He glances at her. She is not looking at him but staring dully in front of her, not hearing a word he is saying*.] Annie! [*She comes to herself with a start*.] Best turn in, Annie, there's a good woman. You ain't well.

MRS. KEENEY [*Resisting his attempts to guide her to*

the door in rear.]   David! Won't you please turn back?

KEENEY [*Gently.*]   I can't, Annie—not yet awhile.
You don't see my meanin'. I got to git the ile.

MRS. KEENEY   It'd be different if you needed the
money, but you don't. You've got more than plenty.

KEENEY [*Impatiently.*]   It ain't the money I'm thinkin' of. D'you think I'm as mean as that?

MRS. KEENEY [*Dully.*]   No—I don't know—I can't
understand—— [*Intensely.*] Oh, I want to be home in the
old house once more and see my own kitchen again, and
hear a woman's voice talking to me and be able to talk to
her. Two years! It seems so long ago—as if I'd been dead
and could never go back.

KEENEY [*Worried by her strange tone and the far-away
look in her eyes.*]   Best go to bed, Annie. You ain't well.

MRS. KEENEY [*Not appearing to hear him.*]   I used to
be lonely when you were away. I used to think Homeport
was a stupid, monotonous place. Then I used to go down
on the beach, especially when it was windy and the break-
ers were rolling in, and I'd dream of the fine free life you
must be leading. [*She gives a laugh which is half a sob.*]
I used to love the sea then. [*She pauses; then continues
with slow intensity.*] But now—I don't ever want to see
the sea again.

KEENEY [*Thinking to humor her.*]   'Tis no fit place
for a woman, that's sure. I was a fool to bring ye.

MRS. KEENEY [*After a pause—passing her hand over
her eyes with a gesture of pathetic weariness.*]   How long
would it take us to reach home—if we started now?

KEENEY [*Frowning.*]   'Bout two months, I reckon,
Annie, with fair luck.

MRS. KEENEY [*Counts on her fingers—then murmurs
with a rapt smile.*]   That would be August, the latter part
of August, wouldn't it? It was on the twenty-fifth of August we were married, David, wasn't it?

KEENEY [*Trying to conceal the fact that her memories
have moved him—gruffly.*]   Don't *you* remember?

MRS. KEENEY [*Vaguely—again passes her hand over
her eyes.*]   My memory is leaving me—up here in the

ice. It was so long ago. [*A pause—then she smiles dreamily.*] It's June now. The lilacs will be all in bloom in the front yard—and the climbing roses on the trellis to the side of the house—they're budding. [*She suddenly covers her face with her hands and commences to sob.*]

KEENEY [*Disturbed.*]   Go in and rest, Annie. You're all wore out cryin' over what can't be helped.

MRS. KEENEY [*Suddenly throwing her arms around his neck and clinging to him.*]   You love me, don't you, David?

KEENEY [*In amazed embarrassment at this outburst.*] Love you? Why d'you ask me such a question, Annie?

MRS. KEENEY [*Shaking him—fiercely.*]   But you do, don't you, David? Tell me!

KEENEY   I'm your husband, Annie, and you're my wife. Could there be aught but love between us after all these years?

MRS. KEENEY [*Shaking him again—still more fiercely.*] Then you do love me. Say it!

KEENEY [*Simply.*]   I do, Annie.

MRS. KEENEY [*Gives a sigh of relief—her hands drop to her sides.* KEENEY *regards her anxiously. She passes her hand across her eyes and murmurs half to herself.*]   I sometimes think if we could only have had a child. [KEENEY *turns away from her, deeply moved. She grabs his arm and turns him around to face her—intensely.*] And I've always been a good wife to you, haven't I, David?

KEENEY [*His voice betraying his emotion.*]   No man has ever had a better, Annie.

MRS. KEENEY   And I've never asked for much from you, have I, David? Have I?

KEENEY   You know you could have all I got the power to give ye, Annie.

MRS. KEENEY [*Wildly.*]   Then do this this once for my sake, for God's sake—take me home! It's killing me, this life—the brutality and cold and horror of it. I'm going mad. I can feel the threat in the air. I can hear the silence threatening me—day after gray day and every day the

same. I can't bear it. [*Sobbing.*] I'll go mad, I know I will.
Take me home, David, if you love me as you say. I'm
afraid. For the love of God, take me home! [*She throws
her arms around him, weeping against his shoulder. His
face betrays the tremendous struggle going on within him.
He holds her out at arm's length, his expression softening.
For a moment his shoulders sag, he becomes old, his iron
spirit weakens as he looks at her tear-stained face.*]

KEENEY [*Dragging out the words with an effort.*]   I'll
do it, Annie—for your sake—if you say it's needful for
ye.

MRS. KEENEY [*With wild joy—kissing him.*]   God
bless you for that, David! [*He turns away from her si-
lently and walks toward the companionway. Just at that
moment there is a clatter of footsteps on the stairs and the
SECOND MATE enters the cabin.*]

MATE [*Excitedly.*]   The ice is breakin' up to no'th'ard,
sir. There's a clear passage through the floe, and clear water beyond, the lookout says.

[KEENEY *straightens himself like a man coming out
of a trance.* MRS. KEENEY *looks at the* MATE *with terrified eyes.*]

KEENEY [*Dazedly—trying to collect his thoughts.*]   A
clear passage? To no'th'ard?

MATE   Yes, sir.

KEENEY [*His voice suddenly grim with determination.*]
Then get her ready and we'll drive her through.

MATE   Aye, aye, sir.

MRS. KEENEY [*Appealingly.*]   David!

KEENEY [*Not heeding her.*]   Will the men turn to willin' or must we drag 'em out?

MATE   They'll turn to willin' enough. You put the fear
o' God into 'em, sir. They're meek as lambs.

KEENEY   Then drive 'em—both watches. [*With grim
determination.*] They's whale t'other side o' this floe and
we're going to git 'em.

MATE   Aye, aye, sir. [*He goes out hurriedly. A moment*

later there is the sound of scuffling feet from the deck out-side and the MATE's *voice shouting orders.*]

KEENEY [*Speaking aloud to himself—derisively.*] And I was agoin' home like a yaller dog!

MRS. KEENEY [*Imploringly.*] David!

KEENEY [*Sternly.*] Woman, you ain't adoin' right when you meddle in men's business and weaken 'em. You can't know my feelin's. I got to prove a man to be a good husband for ye to take pride in. I got to git the ile, I tell ye.

MRS. KEENEY [*Supplicatingly.*] David! Aren't you going home?

KEENEY [*Ignoring this question—commandingly.*] You ain't well. Go and lay down a mite. [*He starts for the door.*] I got to git on deck. [*He goes out. She cries after him in anguish.*] David! [*A pause. She passes her hand across her eyes—then commences to laugh hysterically and goes to the organ. She sits down and starts to play wildly an old hymn.* KEENEY *reënters from the doorway to the deck and stands looking at her angrily. He comes over and grabs her roughly by the shoulder.*]

Woman, what foolish mockin' is this? [*She laughs wildly and he starts back from her in alarm.*] Annie! What is it? [*She doesn't answer him.* KEENEY's *voice trembles.*] Don't you know me, Annie? [*He puts both hands on her shoulders and turns her around so that he can look into her eyes. She stares up at him with a stupid expression, a vague smile on her lips. He stumbles away from her, and she commences softly to play the organ again.*]

[*Swallowing hard—in a hoarse whisper, as if he had difficulty in speaking.*] You said—you was a-goin' mad— God! [*A long wail is heard from the deck above.*] Ah bl-o-o-o-ow! [*A moment later the* MATE's *face appears through the skylight. He cannot see* MRS. KEENEY.]

MATE [*In great excitement.*] Whales, sir—a whole school of 'em—off the starb'd quarter 'bout five miles away—big ones!

KEENEY [*Galvanized into action.*] Are you lowerin' the boats?

MATE Yes, sir.

KEENEY [*With grim decision.*] I'm a-comin' with ye.

MATE Aye, aye, sir. [*Jubilantly.*] You'll git the ile now right enough, sir. [*His head is withdrawn and he can be heard shouting orders.*]

KEENEY [*Turning to his wife.*] Annie! Did you hear him? I'll git the ile. [*She doesn't answer or seem to know he is there. He gives a hard laugh, which is almost a groan.*] I know you're foolin' me, Annie. You ain't out of your mind—[*Anxiously.*] be you? I'll git the ile now right enough—jest a little while longer, Annie—then we'll turn hom'ard. I can't turn back now, you see that, don't ye? I've got to git the ile. [*In sudden terror.*] Answer me! You ain't mad, be you? [*She keeps on playing the organ, but makes no reply. The* MATE's *face appears again through the skylight.*]

MATE All ready, sir. [KEENEY *turns his back on his wife and strides to the doorway, where he stands for a moment and looks back at her in anguish, fighting to control his feelings.*]

Comin', sir?

KEENEY [*His face suddenly grown hard with determination.*] Aye. [*He turns abruptly and goes out.* MRS. KEENEY *does not appear to notice his departure. Her whole attention seems centered in the organ. She sits with half-closed eyes, her body swaying from side to side to the rhythm of the hymn. Her fingers move faster and faster and she is playing wildly and discordantly as*

[CURTAIN]

SOMETHING UNSPOKEN

ΙΝΘΙΩΑΙ

by Tennessee Williams

AFTER the disappointing reception on Broadway of *Orpheus Descending,* Tennessee Williams produced two plays—*Something Unspoken* and *Suddenly Last Summer*—at a small off-Broadway theater under the title *Garden District.* Set in the fashionable "garden district" of New Orleans, these plays were vastly different in mood and construction. *Something Unspoken* was quiet and restrained in tone. *Suddenly Last Summer* was a macabre study of decadence, homosexuality, and cannibalism.

Tennessee Williams has declared, "My longer plays emerge out of earlier one acters or short stories I may have written years before." In the restricted dramatic scope of *Something Unspoken* we can already discern some of the characteristics of the mature playwright. In this concise one acter we find his satirical treatment of Southern mores, his unobtrusive symbolism, his sympathy for the suffering of sensitive people, his poetic dialogue, and his incisive characterization.

CHARACTERS

MISS CORNELIA SCOTT
MISS GRACE LANCASTER

MISS CORNELIA SCOTT, *sixty, a wealthy Southern spinster, is seated at a small mahogany table which is set for two. The other place, not yet occupied, has a single rose in a crystal vase before it.* CORNELIA's *position at the table is flanked by a cradle phone, a silver tray of mail, and an ornate silver coffee urn. An imperial touch is given by purple velvet drapes directly behind her figure at the table. A console phonograph is at the edge of a lighted area.*

At rise of the curtain, she is dialing a number on the phone.

CORNELIA: Is this Mrs. Horton Reid's residence? I am calling for Miss Cornelia Scott. Miss Scott is sorry that she will not be able to attend the meeting of the Confederate Daughters this afternoon as she woke up this morning with a sore throat and has to remain in bed, and will you kindly give her apologies to Mrs. Reid for not letting her know sooner. Thank you. Oh, wait a moment! I think Miss Scott has another message.

[GRACE LANCASTER *enters the lighted area.* CORNELIA *raises her hand in a warning gesture.*]

—What is it, Miss Scott? [*There is a brief pause.*] Oh, Miss Scott would like to leave word for Miss Esmeralda Hawkins to call her as soon as she arrives. Thank you. Good-bye. [*She hangs up.*] You see I am having to impersonate my secretary this morning!

GRACE: The light was so dim it didn't wake me up.

[GRACE *is forty or forty-five, faded but still pretty. Her blonde hair, greying slightly, her pale eyes, her thin figure, in a pink silk dressing gown, give her an insubstantial quality in sharp contrast to* CORNELIA's *Roman gran-*

deur. There is between the two women a mysterious tension, an atmosphere of something unspoken.]

CORNELIA: I've already opened the mail.

GRACE: Anything of interest?

CORNELIA: A card from Thelma Peterson at Mayo's.

GRACE: Oh, how is Thelma?

CORNELIA: She says she's "progressing nicely," whatever that indicates.

GRACE: Didn't she have something removed?

CORNELIA: Several things, I believe.

GRACE: Oh, here's the "Fortnightly Review of Current Letters"!

CORNELIA: Much to my astonishment. I thought I had cancelled my subscription to that publication.

GRACE: Really, Cornelia?

CORNELIA: Surely you remember. I cancelled my subscription immediately after the issue came out with that scurrilous attack on my cousin Cecil Tutwiler Bates, the only dignified novelist the South has produced since Thomas Nelson Page.

GRACE: Oh, yes, I do remember. You wrote a furious letter of protest to the editor of the magazine and you received such a conciliatory reply from an associate editor named Caroline something-or-other that you were completely mollified and cancelled the cancellation.

CORNELIA: I have never been mollified by conciliatory replies, never completely and never even partially, and if I wrote to the editor-in-chief and was answered by an associate editor, my reaction to that piece of impertinence would hardly be what you call "mollified."

GRACE [*changing the subject*]: Oh, here's the new catalogue from the Gramophone Shoppe in Atlanta!

CORNELIA [*conceding a point*]: Yes, there it is.

GRACE: I see you've checked several items.

CORNELIA: I think we ought to build up our collection of Lieder.

GRACE: You've checked a Sibelius that we already have.

CORNELIA: It's getting a little bit scratchy. [*She inhales deeply and sighs, her look fastened upon the silent phone.*] You'll also notice that I've checked a few operatic selections.

GRACE [*excitedly*]: Where, which ones? I don't see them!

CORNELIA: Why are you so excited over the catalogue, dear?

GRACE: I adore phonograph records!

CORNELIA: I wish you adored them enough to put them back in their proper places in albums.

GRACE: Oh, here's the Vivaldi we wanted.

CORNELIA: Not "we," dear. Just you.

GRACE: Not *you*, Cornelia?

CORNELIA: I think Vivaldi's a very thin shadow of Bach.

GRACE: How strange that I should have the impression you . . . [*The phone rings.*] Shall I answer?

CORNELIA: If you will be so kind.

GRACE [*lifting the receiver*]: Miss Scott's residence! [*This announcement is made in a tone of reverence, as though mentioning a seat of holiness.*] Oh, no, no, this is Grace, but Cornelia is right by my side. [*She passes the phone.*] Esmeralda Hawkins.

CORNELIA [*grimly*]: I've been expecting her call. [*Into the phone.*] Hello, Esmeralda, my dear. I've been expecting your call. Now where are you calling me from? Of course I know that you're calling me from the meeting, *ça va sans dire, ma petite!* Ha ha! But from which phone in the house; there's two, you know, the one in the downstairs hall and the one in the chatelaine's boudoir where the ladies will probably be removing their wraps. Oh. You're on the downstairs', are you? Well, by this time I presume that practically all the Daughters have assembled. Now go upstairs and call me back from there so we can talk with a little more privacy, dear, as I want to make my position very clear before the meeting commences. Thank you, dear. [*She hangs up and looks grimly into space.*]

GRACE: The—Confederate Daughters?

CORNELIA: Yes! They're holding the Annual Election today.

GRACE: Oh, how exciting! Why aren't you at the meeting?

CORNELIA: I preferred not to go.

GRACE: You preferred *not* to go?

CORNELIA: Yes, I preferred not to go . . . [*She touches her chest, breathing heavily as if she had run upstairs.*]

GRACE: But it's the annual election of officers.

CORNELIA: Yes! I told you it was!

[GRACE *drops a spoon.* CORNELIA *cries out and jumps a little.*]

GRACE: I'm so sorry. [*She rings the bell for a servant.*]

CORNELIA: Intrigue, intrigue and duplicity revolt me so that I wouldn't be able to breathe in the same atmosphere. [GRACE *rings the bell louder.*] Why are you ringing that bell? You know Lucinda's not here!

GRACE: I'm so sorry. Where has Lucinda gone?

CORNELIA [*in a hoarse whisper, barely audible*]: There's a big colored funeral in town. [*She clears her throat violently and repeats the statement.*]

GRACE: Oh, dear. You have that nervous laryngitis.

CORNELIA: No sleep, no sleep last night.

[*The phone screams at her elbow. She cries out and thrusts it from her as if it were on fire.*]

GRACE [*picking up the phone*]: Miss Scott's residence. Oh. Just a moment, please.

CORNELIA [*snatching the phone*]: Esmeralda, are you upstairs now?

GRACE [*in a loud whisper*]: It isn't Esmeralda, it's Mrs. C. C. Bright!

CORNELIA: One moment, one moment, one moment! [*She thrusts the phone back at* GRACE *with a glare of fury.*] How dare you put me on the line with that woman!

GRACE: Cornelia, I didn't, I was just going to ask you if you . . .

CORNELIA: *Hush!* [*She springs back from the table, glaring across it.*] Now give me that phone. [*She takes it, and says coldly.*] What can I do for you, please? No. I'm afraid that my garden will not be open to the Pilgrims this spring. I think the cultivation of gardens is an esthetic hobby and not a competitive sport. Individual visitors will be welcome if they call in advance so that I can arrange for my gardener to show them around, but no bands of Pilgrims, not after the devastation my garden suffered last spring—Pilgrims coming with dogs—picking flowers and . . . You're entirely welcome; yes, good-bye. [*She returns the phone to* GRACE.]

GRACE: I think the election would have been less of a strain if you'd gone to it, Cornelia.

CORNELIA: I don't know what you are talking about.

GRACE: Aren't you up for office?

CORNELIA: "Up for office?" What is "up for office"?

GRACE: Why, ha ha! *running* for—something.

CORNELIA: Have you ever known me to *"run"* for anything, Grace? Whenever I've held an office in a society or club it's been at the *insistence* of the members because I really have an *aversion* to holding office. But this is a different thing, a different thing altogether. It's a test of something. You see I have known for some time, now, that there is a little group, a *clique*, in the Daughters, which is hostile to me.

GRACE: Oh, Cornelia, I'm sure you must be mistaken.

CORNELIA: No. There is a movement against me.

GRACE: A movement? A movement against you?

CORNELIA: An organized movement to keep me out of any important office.

GRACE: But haven't you always held some important office in the Chapter?

CORNELIA: I have never been *Regent* of it.

GRACE: Oh, you want to be *Regent?*

CORNELIA: No. You misunderstand me. I don't *"want"* to be Regent.

GRACE: Oh?

CORNELIA: I don't "want" to be anything whatsoever. I simply want to break up this movement against me and for that purpose I have rallied my forces.

GRACE: Your forces? [*Her lips twitch slightly as if she had an hysterical impulse to smile.*]

CORNELIA: Yes. I still have some friends in the Chapter who have resisted the movement.

GRACE: Oh?

CORNELIA: I have the solid support of all the older Board members.

GRACE: Why, then, I should think you'd have nothing to worry about.

CORNELIA: The Chapter has expanded too rapidly lately. Women have been admitted that couldn't get into a front pew at the Second Baptist Church! And that's the disgraceful truth . . .

GRACE: But since it's really a patriotic society . . .

CORNELIA: My dear Grace, there are two chapters of the Confederate Daughters in the city of Meridian. There is the Forrest chapter, which is for social riff-raff, and there is *this* chapter which was *supposed* to have a *little* bit of *distinction!* I'm not a snob. I'm nothing if not democratic. You know *that!* But . . .

[*The phone rings.* CORNELIA *reaches for it, then pushes it to* GRACE.]

GRACE: Miss Scott's residence! Oh, yes, yes, just a moment! [*She passes phone to* CORNELIA.] It's Esmeralda Hawkins.

CORNELIA [*into the phone*]: Are you upstairs now, dear? Well, I wondered, it took you so long to call back. Oh, but I thought you said the luncheon was over. Well. I'm glad that you fortified yourself with a bite to eat. What did the buffet consist of? Chicken à la king! Wouldn't you know it! That is so characteristic of poor Amelia! With bits of pimiento and tiny mushrooms in it? What did the ladies counting their calories do? Nibbled around the edges? Oh, poor dears!—and afterwards I suppose there was lemon sherbet with lady-fingers? What, lime sherbet! And *no* lady-fingers? *What a departure!* What a *shocking* apostasy! I'm quite stunned! Ho ho ho . . . [*She reaches shakily for her cup.*] Now what's going on? Discussing the Civil Rights Program? Then they won't take the vote for at least half an hour! Now Esmeralda, I *do* hope that you understand my position clearly.

I don't wish to hold any office in the chapter unless it's by acclamation. You know what that means, don't you? It's a parliamentary term. It means when someone is desired for an office so unanimously that no vote has to be taken. In other words, elected automatically, simply by nomination, unopposed. Yes, my dear, it's just as simple as that. I have served as Treasurer for three terms, twice as Secretary, once as Chaplain—and what a dreary office that was with those long-drawn prayers for the Confederate dead! Altogether I've served on the Board for, let's see, fourteen years! Well, now, my dear, the point is simply this. If Daughters feel that I have demonstrated my capabilities and loyalty strongly enough that I should simply be named as Regent without a vote being taken— by unanimous acclamation!—why, then, of course I would feel obliged to accept. [*Her voice trembles with emotion.*] But if, on the other hand, the—uh—*clique!*—and you know the ones I mean!—is bold enough to propose someone else for the office . . . Do you understand my position? In that eventuality, hard as it is to imagine, I prefer to bow out of the picture entirely! The moment another nomination is made and seconded, my own must be withdrawn, at once, unconditionally! Is that quite understood, Esmeralda? Then good! Go back downstairs to the meeting. Digest your chicken à la king, my dear, and call me again on the upstairs phone as soon as there's something to tell me.

[*She hangs up and stares grimly into space.* GRACE *lifts a section of grapefruit on a tiny silver fork.*]

GRACE: They haven't had it yet?

CORNELIA: Had what, dear?

GRACE: The election!

CORNELIA: No, not yet. It seems to be—imminent, though.

GRACE: Cornelia, why don't you think about something else until it's over?

CORNELIA: What makes you think that I am nervous about it?

GRACE: You're—you're *breathing* so fast.

CORNELIA: I didn't sleep well last night. You were prowling about the house with that stitch in your side.

GRACE: I *am* so sorry. You know it's nothing. A muscular contraction that comes from strain.

CORNELIA: What strain does it come from, Grace?

GRACE: What strain? [*She utters a faint, perplexed laugh.*] Why!—I don't know . . .

CORNELIA: The strain of *what?* Would you like *me* to tell you?

GRACE [*rising*]: Excuse me, I . . .

CORNELIA [*sharply*]: Where are you going?

GRACE: Upstairs for a moment! I just remembered I should have taken my drops of belladonna!

CORNELIA: It does no good *after* eating.

GRACE: I suppose that's right. It doesn't.

CORNELIA: But you want to escape?

GRACE: Of course not.

CORNELIA: Several times lately you've rushed away from me as if I'd suddenly threatened you with a knife.

GRACE: Cornelia! I've been—jumpy!

CORNELIA: It's always when something is almost—*spoken*—between us.

GRACE: I hate to see you so agitated over the outcome of a silly club-woman's election.

CORNELIA: I'm not talking about the Daughters. I'm not even thinking about them, I'm . . .

GRACE: I wish you'd dismiss it completely from your mind. Now would be a good time to play some records. Let me put a symphony on the machine!

CORNELIA: No.

GRACE: How about the Bach for Piano and Strings? The one we received for Christmas from Jessie and Gay?

CORNELIA: "No," I said; "No," I said. No!

GRACE: Something very light and quiet, then, the old French madrigals, maybe?

CORNELIA: Anything to avoid a talk between us? Anything to evade a conversation, especially when the servant is not in the house?

GRACE: Oh, here it is! This is just the thing! [*She has*

started the phonograph. Landowska is playing a harpsi-
chord selection. The phonograph is at the edge of the
lighted area or just outside it. CORNELIA *stares grimly as*
GRACE *resumes her seat with an affectation of enchant-*
ment, clasping her hands and closing her eyes. She speaks
in an enchanted voice.] Oh, how it smooths things over,
how sweet, and gentle, and—pure.

CORNELIA: Yes! And completely dishonest.

GRACE: Music? Dishonest?

CORNELIA: Completely. It "smooths things over" instead of—speaking them out.

GRACE: "Music hath charms to soothe the savage
breast."

CORNELIA: Yes, oh, yes, if the savage breast permits it.

GRACE: Oh, sublime—sublime!

CORNELIA [*grudgingly*]: Landowska is an artist of rare
precision.

GRACE [*ecstatically*]: And such a noble face, a profile
as fine and strong as Edith Sitwell's. After this we'll play
Edith Sitwell's *Façade*. "Jane, Jane, tall as a crane, the
morning light creaks down again . . ."

CORNELIA: Dearest, isn't there something you've failed
to notice?

GRACE: Where?

CORNELIA: Right under your nose.

GRACE: Oh! You mean my flower?

CORNELIA: Yes! I mean your rose.

GRACE: Of course I noticed my rose; the moment I came
in the room I saw it here.

CORNELIA: You made no allusion to it.

GRACE: I would have, but you were so concerned over
the meeting.

CORNELIA: I'm not concerned over the meeting.

GRACE: Whom do I have to thank for this lovely rose?
My gracious employer?

CORNELIA: You will find fourteen others on your desk
in the library when you go in to take care of the corre-
spondence.

GRACE: Fourteen other roses?

CORNELIA: A total of fifteen!

GRACE: How wonderful! Why fifteen?

CORNELIA: How long have you been here, dearest? How long have you made this house a house of roses?

GRACE: What a nice way to put it! Why, of course! I've been your secretary for fifteen years.

CORNELIA: Fifteen years my companion! A rose for every year, a year for every rose!

GRACE: What a charming sort of way to—observe the—occasion.

CORNELIA: First I thought "pearls" and then I thought, No, roses, but perhaps I should have given you something golden, ha ha! Silence is golden, they say.

GRACE: Oh, dear, that stupid machine is playing the same record over.

CORNELIA: Let it, let it; I like it.

GRACE: Just let me . . .

CORNELIA: Sit down!—It was fifteen years ago this very morning, on the sixth day of November, that someone very sweet and gentle and silent—a shy, little, quiet little widow!—arrived for the first time at Seven Edgewater Drive. The season was autumn. I had been raking dead leaves over the rose-bushes to protect them from frost when I heard footsteps on the gravel; light, quick, delicate footsteps like spring coming in the middle of autumn; and looked up, and sure enough, there spring was! A little person so thin that light shone through her as if she were made of the silk of a white parasol! [GRACE *utters a short, startled laugh. Wounded,* CORNELIA *speaks harshly.*] Why did you laugh? Why did you laugh like that?

GRACE: It sounded—ha ha!—it sounded like the first paragraph of a woman's magazine story.

CORNELIA: What a cutting remark!

GRACE: I didn't mean it that way, I . . .

CORNELIA: What other way could you mean it?

GRACE: Cornelia, you know how I am! I'm always a little embarrassed by sentiment, aren't I?

CORNELIA: Yes, frightened of anything that betrays some feeling.

GRACE: People who don't know you well, nearly all people we know, would be astounded to hear you, Cornelia Scott, that grave and dignified lady, expressing herself in such a lyrical manner.

CORNELIA: People who don't know me well are everybody! Yes, I think even *you!*

GRACE: Cornelia, you must admit that sentiment isn't like you.

CORNELIA: *Is nothing like me but silence?* [*The clock ticks loudly.*] *Am I sentenced to silence for a lifetime?*

GRACE: It's just not like you to . . .

CORNELIA: Not like me, not like me; what do you know what's like me or not like me?

GRACE: You may deny it, Cornelia, as much as you please, but it's evident to me that you are completely unstrung by your anxieties over the Confederate Daughters' election.

CORNELIA: Another thinly veiled insult?

GRACE: Oh, Cornelia, please!

CORNELIA [*imitating her gesture*]: "Oh, Cornelia, please!!"

GRACE: If I've said anything wrong, I beg your pardon. I offer my very humble apologies for it.

CORNELIA: I don't want apologies from you.

[*There is a strained silence. The clock ticks. Suddenly* GRACE *reaches across to touch the veined jewelled hand of* CORNELIA. CORNELIA *snatches her own hand away as though the touch had burned her.*]

GRACE: Thank you for the roses.

CORNELIA: I don't want thanks from you either. All that I want is a little return of affection, not much, but sometimes a little.

GRACE: You have that always, Cornelia.

CORNELIA: And one thing more: a little outspokenness, too.

GRACE: Outspokenness?

CORNELIA: Yes, outspokenness, if that's not too much to ask from such a proud young lady.

GRACE [*rising from the table*]: I am not proud and I am not young, Cornelia.

CORNELIA: Sit down! Don't leave the table!

GRACE: Is that an order?

CORNELIA: I don't give orders to you; I make requests.

GRACE: Sometimes the requests of an employer are hard to distinguish from orders. [*She sits down.*]

CORNELIA: Please turn off the victrola. [GRACE *rises and stops the machine.*] Grace!—Don't you feel there's—*something unspoken* between us?

GRACE: No. No, I don't.

CORNELIA: I do. I've felt for a long time something unspoken between us.

GRACE: Don't you think there is always something unspoken between two people?

CORNELIA: I see no reason for it.

GRACE: But don't a great many things exist without reason?

CORNELIA: Let's not turn this into a metaphysical discussion.

GRACE: All right. But you mystify me.

CORNELIA: It's very simple. It's just that I feel that there's something unspoken between us that ought to be spoken. . . . Why are you looking at me like that?

GRACE: How am I looking at you?

CORNELIA: With positive terror!

GRACE: Cornelia!

CORNELIA: You are, you are, but I'm not going to be shut up.

GRACE: Go on, continue, please, do!

CORNELIA: I'm going to, I will, I will, I . . . [*The phone rings and* GRACE *reaches for it.*] No, no, no, let it ring! [*It goes on ringing.*] Take it off the hook!

GRACE: Do just let me . . .

CORNELIA: Off the hook, I told you!

[GRACE *takes the phone off the hook. A voice says:* "Hello? Hello? Hello? Hello?"]

GRACE [*suddenly sobbing*]: I can't stand it!

CORNELIA: *Be* STILL*! Someone can hear you!*

VOICE: Hello? Hello? Cornelia? Cornelia Scott?

[CORNELIA *seizes the phone and slams it back into its cradle.*]

CORNELIA: Now stop that! Stop that silly little female trick!

GRACE: You say there's something unspoken. Maybe there is. I don't know. But I do know some things are better left unspoken. Also I know that when a silence between two people has gone on for a long time, it's like a wall that's impenetrable between them. Maybe between us there is such a wall. One that's impenetrable. Or maybe *you* can break it. I know I can't. I can't even attempt to. You're the strong one of us two and surely you know it. Both of us have turned grey!—But not the same kind of grey. In that velvet dressing-gown you look like the Emperor Tiberius!—In his imperial toga! Your hair and your eyes are both the color of iron! Iron grey. Invincible looking! People nearby are all somewhat—frightened of you. They feel your force and they admire you for it. They come to you here for opinions on this or that. What plays are good on Broadway this season, what books are worth reading and what books are trash and what—what records are valuable and—what is the proper attitude toward— bills in Congress! Oh, you're a fountain of wisdom! And in addition to that, you have your—*wealth!* Yes, you have your—*fortune!* All of your real-estate holdings, your blue-chip stocks, your—bonds, your—mansion on Edgewater Drive, your—shy little—secretary, your—fabulous gardens that Pilgrims cannot go into . . .

CORNELIA: Oh, yes, now you are speaking, now you are speaking at last! Go on, please go on speaking.

GRACE: I am—very—different! Also turning grey, but my grey is different. Not iron, like yours, not imperial, Cornelia, but grey, yes, grey, the color of a . . . *cobweb* . . . [*She starts the record again, very softly.*] Something white getting soiled, the grey of something forgotten. [*The phone rings again. Neither of them seems to notice it.*] And that being the case, that being the difference between our two kinds of grey, yours and mine, you mustn't expect me to give bold answers to questions that make the house shake with silence! To speak out things that are fifteen years unspoken!—That long a time can make a silence a wall that nothing less than dynamite could break through and [*She picks up the phone.*] I'm not strong enough, bold enough, I'm not . . .

CORNELIA [*fiercely*]: You're speaking into the phone!

GRACE [*into phone*]: Hello? Oh, yes, she's here. It's Esmeralda Hawkins.

[CORNELIA *snatches the phone.*]

CORNELIA: What is it, Esmeralda? What are you saying; is the room full of women? Such a babble of voices! What are you trying to tell me? Have they held the election already? What, what, what? Oh, this is maddening! I can't hear a word that you're saying, it sounds like the Fourth of July, a great celebration! Ha, ha, now try once more with your mouth closer to the phone! What, what? Would I be willing to what? You can't be serious! Are you out of your mind? [*She speaks to* GRACE *in a panicky voice.*] She wants to know if I would be willing to serve *as vice-*Regent! [*Into phone.*] Esmeralda! Will you listen to me? What's going on? Are there some fresh defections? How does it look? Why did you call me again before the vote? Louder, please speak louder, and cup your mouth to the phone in case they're eavesdropping! Who asked if I would accept the vice-regency, dear? Oh, Mrs. Colby, of course!—that treacherous witch! *Esmeralda!! Listen I—will accept—no office—except—the highest!* Did you understand that? *I—will accept no office except—*ESME-RALDA! [*She drops the phone into its cradle.*]

GRACE: Have they held the election?

CORNELIA [*dazed*]: What? No, there's a five-minute recess before the election begins.

GRACE: Things are not going well?

CORNELIA: "Would you accept the vice-regency," she asked me, "if for some reason they don't elect you Regent?" Then she hung up as if somebody had snatched the phone away from her, or the house had—caught fire.

GRACE: You shouted so I think she must have been frightened.

CORNELIA: Whom can you trust in this world; whom can you ever rely on?

GRACE: I think perhaps you should have gone to the meeting.

CORNELIA: I think my not being there is much more pointed.

GRACE [*rising again*]: May I be excused, now?

CORNELIA: No! Stay here!

GRACE: If that is just a request, I . . .

CORNELIA: That's an order! [GRACE *sits down and closes her eyes.*] When you first came to this house, do you know I didn't expect you?

GRACE: Oh, but, Cornelia, you'd invited me here.

CORNELIA: We hardly knew each other.

GRACE: We'd met the summer before when Ralph was . . .

CORNELIA: Living! Yes, we met at Sewanee where he was a summer instructor.

GRACE: He was already ill.

CORNELIA: I thought what a pity that lovely, delicate girl hasn't found someone she could lean on, who could protect her! And two months later I heard through Clarabelle Drake that he was dead.

GRACE: You wrote me such a sweet letter, saying how lonely you were since the loss of your mother and urging me to rest here till the shock was over. You seemed to understand how badly I needed to withdraw for a while from—old associations. I hesitated to come. I didn't until you wrote me a second letter . . .

CORNELIA: After I received yours. You wanted urging.

GRACE: I wanted to be quite sure I was really wanted. I only came intending to stay a few weeks. I was so afraid that I would outstay my welcome.

CORNELIA: How blind of you not to see how desperately I wanted to keep you here forever.

GRACE: Oh, I did see that you—[*The phone rings.*] Miss Scott's residence! Yes, she's here.

CORNELIA [*snatching the phone finally*]: Cornelia Scott speaking! Oh. It's you, Esmeralda! Well, how did it come out? *I don't believe you! I simply don't believe you!* [GRACE *sits down quietly at the table.*] *Mrs. Hornsby elected?* Well, there's a dark horse for you! Less than a year in the Chapter . . . Did you—nominate—*me?* Oh, I see! But I told you to withdraw my name if . . . No, no, no, don't explain; it doesn't matter; I have too much already. You know I am going into the Daughters of the Barons of Runnymede. Yes, it's been established, I have a direct line to the Earl of . . . No, it's been straight-ened out; a clear line is established, and then of course I am also eligible for the Colonial Dames and for the Huguenot Society; and what with all my other activities and so forth, why, I couldn't *possibly* have taken it on if they'd—*wanted* . . . Of course I'm going to resign from the local chapter! Oh, yes, I am! My secretary is sitting right here by me. She has her pencil, her notebook! I'm going to dictate my letter of resignation from the local chapter the moment that I hang up on this conversation. Oh, no, no, no, I'm not mad, not outraged, at all. I'm just a little—ha ha!—a little—amused . . . *Mrs. Hornsby?* Nothing succeeds like mediocrity, does it? Thanks and good-bye, Esmeralda. [*She hangs up, stunned.* GRACE *rises.*]

GRACE: Notebook and pencil?

CORNELIA: Yes. Notebook and pencil. I have to—dic-tate a letter.

[GRACE *leaves the table. Just at the edge of the lighted area, she turns to glance at* CORNELIA'S *rigid shoulders, and a slight, equivocal smile appears momentarily on her face; not quite malicious but not really sympathetic. Then she crosses out of the light. A moment later, her voice comes from the outer dark.*]

GRACE: What lovely roses! One for every year!

CURTAIN

TO BOBOLINK,
FOR HER SPIRIT

by William Inge

IN THE FOREWORD to a collection of his plays, William Inge wrote: "I regard a play as a composition rather than a story, as a distillation of life rather than a narration of it." *To Bobolink, For Her Spirit* is an excellent illustration of Inge's artistic credo. Beneath its humorous surface we sense the pathetic groping of "little people" who strive to catch a fleeting glimpse of an artificial glamor world created by modern mass media forms of entertainment. As an escape from the dull world of reality, Bobolink and the teen-agers idolize the ephemeral celebrities created by commercialism. These entertainers, themselves exploited for profit, in turn exploit the adulation of their fans eager to enter a world of romantic illusion. Patiently the unglamorous group await the appearance of their publicized idol, to win a nod of recognition or to gain a coveted autograph.

CHARACTERS

RENALDO   BOBOLINK
FRITZ   GRETCHEN
NELLIE   ANNAMARIE

Every day the weather permits, a group of autograph hunters assembles outside the 21 Club in New York. The size of the group varies from day to day and seems to depend upon the number and magnitude of the movie stars reported to be inside. It is an oddly assorted group, most of them teen-agers, but sometimes middle-aged women are included. The ringleader of today's group is BOBOLINK BOWEN, *a woman probably in her early thirties, who is so fat that her body, in silhouette, would form an almost perfect circle.* BOBOLINK *has the fat woman's usual disposition, stolidly complacent and happy. Her lips usually are formed in a grin of guzzling contentment. Her hair is short and kinky; she wears thick-lensed glasses that reduce her eyes to the size of buttonholes, and her clothes by necessity are simple: a man's coat-style sweater, saddle shoes and bobbysocks and bare legs that swell at the calves like bowling pins.* NELLIE, *a starved and eager woman in her late twenties, is* BOBOLINK's *dependable stand-by. The two young boys,* RENALDO *and* FRITZ, *are friends; the two young girls,* GRETCHEN *and* ANNAMARIE, *are friends also. They are people without any personal attraction they could possibly lay claim to, and so must find in others attributes they want and lack in themselves.* ANNA-MARIE, *in her dress, has tried to emulate one of her favorite film stars; she wears exotic sun glasses, a complicated coiffure and exciting shoes with straps, bows and platform soles. The group has been standing around for over an hour. They have learned to handle these periods of waiting like patients in a rest*

home; they talk idly with one another, move rest-
lessly about in a limited space. GRETCHEN *knits,*
FRITZ *is working a crossword puzzle. Behind them*
stands the DOORMAN, *a man of rigid and calculated*
dignity, dressed in a colorful uniform. He holds his
head high and keeps it turned away from the auto-
graph seekers as though to disclaim any association
with them.

RENALDO   I heard Lana Turner was in this joint last
week. Man, wouldn't that be something?

FRITZ   Just imagine walking down the street one day
and . . . plop! all of a sudden there's Lana Turner . . .
just outa the blue. Man, I'd drop my teeth.

NELLIE (*Making a claim that* BOBOLINK *would be too
proud to make for herself*)   Bobolink here's got Lana
Turner's autograph. Haven't you, Bobby?

BOBOLINK   Lana's no better'n anyone else.

FRITZ (*Impressed; to* BOBOLINK)   No foolin'? You got
Lana Turner's autograph?

BOBOLINK (*Proving it with her autograph book*)
Think I was lying to you?

FRITZ (*To* RENALDO)   Look, Ronny, she's got it.

NELLIE   Oh, Bobolink's got 'em all.

BOBOLINK (*She always holds her own*)   I got all of 'em
that's worth gettin'.

GRETCHEN   My girl friend saw her. My girl friend goes
out to California every summer. Her folks are real
wealthy. She saw Lana Turner on the beach one day and
she just goes up to her and says, "Hi, Lana" . . . just
like that. And Lana smiles back and says, "Hi!"

BOBOLINK   Sure, she's not stuck-up. Now Katharine
Hepburn's stuck-up, but Lana Turner's not at all. The
best ones never are stuck-up.

FRITZ (*Addressing the* DOORMAN, *who stands with rigid
dignity*)   Hey, mister, how long's Perry Como been inside?

(*The* DOORMAN *does not respond*)

BOBOLINK (*To* FRITZ)   Hey, don't you know anything?
Those guys don't pay no attention to movie stars. They
see so many of 'em they get sick of 'em. You can't find out
anything from him.

FRITZ   Are we sure Perry Como's there?

BOBOLINK (*Impatiently*)   I told you I seen him, didn't
I? Well, what more do you want? I was up there on the
corner waitin' for a bus. Nellie here nudges me and says,
"Hey, ain't that Perry Como goin' into the 21 Club?" And
I looked and sure enough. There was a guy goin' in, had
on the same kinda suit Perry Como had on last week over
at the Paramount. Looked exactly like him.

FRITZ   But are you sure it was him?

BOBOLINK   Look, boy, you're never sure of anything
in this world, don't you know that?

FRITZ   We been waiting here over an hour.

BOBOLINK   No one's asking you to stay. I waited outside the Stork Club three hours one night, three whole
hours, and it was snowin'. Someone told me Elizabeth
Taylor was inside and I wanted her autograph. It wasn't
Elizabeth Taylor at all. Just some college girl trying to
make out she was Elizabeth Taylor. I was sore, but what
the heck!

NELLIE   Besides, you never know what's going to hap-
pen in this racket; like the time we was waitin' outside the
St. Regis for Ronald Colman, and shoot! Who cares about
Ronald Colman . . .

RENALDO   He's famous.

NELLIE   Not very. Anyway, we was waitin' for his autograph and . . .

BOBOLINK (*Taking over*)   Oh, yeh, and we'd been waiting 1or Ronald Colman all night and we was just about
to give up and go home and then what do you think happened?

(*She's going to build up suspense by making them guess*)

NELLIE   That was the best luck we ever had, wasn't it, Bobby?

BOBOLINK   Well, we was just about to give up and go home when a taxi draws up at the curb and Van Johnson and Peter Lawford get out, and we got 'em both, right there on the same spot.

(*This is an impressive story. The others are a little awed*)

GRETCHEN   No foolin'! You got Van Johnson and Peter Lawford?

BOBOLINK (*She produces her autograph book proudly*) And both at the same time!

NELLIE (*Producing her own evidence*)   I got 'em, too.

BOBOLINK   See what Peter Lawford wrote? "All my love to Bobolink." I told him that was my name.

NELLIE   And he said the same thing on mine, but my name's Nellie. They're both just as cute in real life as they are in pictures, aren't they, Bobby?

BOBOLINK   Not a bit stuck-up.

(*An elaborately dressed couple appears in the doorway coming out of the restaurant. The woman wears a dress of dramatic cut and an exotic hat. Their manner is ridiculously aloof and they make quite a thing of ignoring the autograph hounds*)

FRITZ (*Nudging* RENALDO)   Hey, who's that?

(*They all look*)

GRETCHEN   Looks like Rosalind Russell, don't it?

BOBOLINK   Naw, that ain't Rosalind Russell. I seen Rosalind Russell. She's real tall.

ANNAMARIE   Isn't she stunning? Don't you just love that dress?

GRETCHEN   I bet that dress cost two or three hundred dollars.

ANNAMARIE   'Course it did. Probably cost more than that.

(BOBOLINK *is studying the woman, trying to decide who she is. The woman and her escort now stand at the curb waiting for the* DOORMAN *to hail them a cab. The hounds are gaping at them*)

FRITZ (*Approaching the glamorous woman*)   Miss, can I have your autograph?

(*The woman is a little surprised. She looks questioningly at her escort, who gives her an indulgent smile. So the woman, a little mystified, signs her name to* FRITZ's *book. Then she and her escort disappear in a cab.* FRITZ *studies the signature. The others flock around him to see who it is, but* BOBOLINK *is not as quickly curious as the others*)

ALL   Who is she? Hey, let's see. It's not Rosalind Russell, is it? If I missed Rosalind Russell, I could kill myself. Let's see.

FRITZ   I'm trying to make it out. (*He attempts a pronunciation of the name*) Irina Nechibidikoff.

BOBOLINK (*Emphatically*)   Russian!

FRITZ   Hey, she may be someone famous.

BOBOLINK   Whoever heard of Irina Nechibidikoff?

ANNAMARIE   Maybe she's a famous dancer.

BOBOLINK   So what? She's not in the movies, is she? With a name like that.

GRETCHEN   Maybe she's a famous singer.

FRITZ   Anyway, I got her, whoever she is.

BOBOLINK   I'm waitin' here for Perry Como. I come for Perry Como, and I'm gonna stay till I *get* Perry Como.

NELLIE (*To the others*) Bobby always finishes up what she starts out to do.

BOBOLINK You tell the world I do. And I'm not leavin' here without Perry Como's autograph. I been trailin' him for two years. I got Bing Crosby; I got Frank Sinatra; I got Van Johnson and Peter Lawford and Jimmy Stewart and Tyrone Power . . .

NELLIE Tell 'em about the time you got Tyrone Power, Bobby.

BOBOLINK Now I mean to get Perry Como. He's not my favorite or anything, but I want to get his autograph.

NELLIE Tyrone Power's your real favorite, isn't he, Bobolink?

BOBOLINK (*With modest adoration*) Yah. Tyrone's a real guy.

NELLIE (*To the others*) Bobbie's president of the Tyrone Power Fan Club up in Irvington. (*The others are impressed*) Go on, Bobbie, tell 'em about Tyrone.

BOBOLINK (*This is too sacred to be treated lightly and* BOBOLINK *is capable of dramatizing her modesty*) No, Nellie, I don't think it's right a person should go around boasting about things like that.

NELLIE Tell 'em, Bobby. If you don', I will. (BOBOLINK, *after all, can't stop her*) Bobby's too modest about it, I think. But Tyrone Power shook her hand and told her personally that he was very indebted to her . . .

BOBOLINK I met him at the train; don't forget that, Nellie.

NELLIE As president of the Tyrone Power Fan Club in Irvington, she met his train at the Pennsylvania Station when he came in from Hollywood.

BOBOLINK And I had to fight the man at the gate to let me pass.

NELLIE That's right. She did. See, it wasn't supposed to be known that Tyrone was on that train, but the Pasadena Fan Club had wired us he was coming, so Bobby and I met him at the train to welcome him to New York, didn't we, Bobby?

BOBOLINK   We didn't want him t'arrive in town all alone.

NELLIE   'Course not. So we went down to the station together. The man at the gate wouldn't let us through, but Bobby got by him, didn't you, Bobby? I had to stay behind, but Bobby got through and got right on the train, didn't you, Bobby?

BOBOLINK   And I hunted all through them cars till I found him. He was still packing his things and he was in a hurry.

NELLIE   But he wasn't stuck-up, was he, Bobby?

BOBOLINK   (*This is sacred to her*)   No, he wasn't stuck-up at all. I introduced myself as the president of the Irvington Fan Club, and told him we had forty-three members and met once a week to discuss his career.

NELLIE   And he was very pleased, wasn't he, Bobby?

BOBOLINK   Of course he was. And I told him us fans was awful glad he didn't marry Lana Turner 'cause, although our club don't have anything personal against Lana Turner, we never did think she was the right sort for Tyrone. And I told him that in just those words.

NELLIE   And she isn't. I mean, I like Lana Turner and I think she's awfully pretty and of course she's awful famous, but she isn't the right sort of girl for Tyrone at all.

GRETCHEN   And you got his autograph?

BOBOLINK   'Course I got his autograph, silly. Nellie did, too. And he gave me lots of his autographs to give to other club members, but he made me promise not to give them to anyone else. (*She displays her proudest acquisition*)   Just club members. Then he told me to call him Tyrone, and he said he was very indebted to me. See what he wrote?

FRITZ   (*Reading the inscription aloud*)   "To Bobolink, for her faithful enthusiasm and spirit." Gee!

BOBOLINK   Then he had his secretary give me a picture and he autographed it, too. It just says, "With gratitude, Tyrone." Then he shook my hand and he said he wished he could come to Irvington to visit the fan club, but he was going to be terribly busy in New York, he wouldn't have a minute to spare, and then he had to get back to Hollywood to make another picture.

ANNAMARIE (*To* NELLIE)   Did you meet him?

NELLIE   No, but I saw him. He came hurrying through the gate with his coat collar turned up so no one would recognize him. I called out, "Hi, Tyrone! I'm a friend of Bobolink," but he started running.

BOBOLINK   He didn't want people to know who he was. Sometimes they get mobbed by fans and get their clothes ripped off and even get hurt. I wouldn't want anything like that to happen to Tryone.

(*Another couple appear in entrance way. The young man is dapper and handsome and the girl is pretty and expensively dressed. The haughty* DOORMAN *starts hailing a cab*)

RENALDO   Hey, who's this?

GRETCHEN   Is this Perry Como?

BOBOLINK (*With a look*)   No, that ain't Perry Como.

NELLIE   She looks familiar, don't she? I bet she's in pictures.

BOBOLINK (*After a moment's study*)   No, she ain't in pictures.

FRITZ   They might be somebody. They might be somebody we haven't heard about yet. (*The couple stand at the curb now.* FRITZ *approaches them*) Mister, can I have your autograph?

ANNAMARIE (*To the girl*)   Are you in pictures?

(*The girl smiles tolerantly and shakes her head no*)

GRETCHEN   Go on and sign anyway, will you please?

ANNAMARIE   I bet you're both in pictures and just don't wanta admit it. C'mon and give us your autograph.

(*The young man and the girl smile at each other and sign the books, while the* DOORMAN *hails a cab. But*

this is small-time stuff for BOBOLINK. *She has the dignity of her past career to think of. She stays back,
leaning against the grill fence surrounding the club,
with a look of superior calm on her face.* NELLIE *stays
by her side*)

NELLIE   I don't think they're anyone famous, do you,
Bobolink?

BOBOLINK   'Course not. I can tell the famous ones. I
can tell.

NELLIE   Sure you can, Bobby.

(*The couple go off in a cab. The* DOORMAN *returns
to his position by the doorway. The young autograph
seekers start studying the names that have been in-
scribed in their books*)

BOBOLINK   They might be famous *one* day . . . I said
they *might* be . . . But I don't have time to waste on people that *might* be famous.

NELLIE   'Course not.

(*They stand quietly, removed from the others now*)

FRITZ   (*Reading his new acquisitions*)   Frederick
Bischoff and Mary Milton. Who are they?

ANNAMARIE   Yah, who are they?

GRETCHEN   I bet she models. I think I seen her picture
once in an ad for hair remover. Yah, that was her. I know
it was. It was a picture showed her with one arm stretched
over her head so you could see she didn't have no hair
under her arm and was smiling real pretty.

ANNAMARIE   He's probably just a model, too. He was
kinda cute, though.

BOBOLINK   (*Personally to* NELLIE, *in appraisal of her
colleagues*)   These are just kids, Nellie.

NELLIE   Yah.

FRITZ   Isn't anyone famous ever coming outa there?

RENALDO (*To* BOBOLINK)   Are you sure you saw Perry Como go inside?

BOBOLINK   I said Perry Como was inside, didn't I? If you don't believe me, you don't have to.

NELLIE   Bobolink knows a lot more about these things than you kids do. She spotted Perry Como two blocks away and Bobolink don't make mistakes.

RENALDO   O.K. O.K. Don't get sore.

NELLIE   You might remember that Bobolink is president of the Tyrone Power Fan Club.

FRITZ   We wasn't doubtin' your word. C'mon, Renaldo. Let's wait.

GRETCHEN   Let's wait a little longer, Annamarie.

ANNAMARIE   I gotta get home for supper, Gretchen.

GRETCHEN   Let's wait.

FRITZ (*To* RENALDO)   Let's wait.

(*They resume their positions of patient attendance*)

CURTAIN

THE FEAST

by Daniel Wright

Author's Note

The Feast, it must be mentioned, was written with a particular performance situation in mind—a situation in which this play was to be one of several short plays produced before an audience. In this sense it is a self-conscious play; it seems to comment upon the nature of drama. It seems to make fun not only of its own inherent pretense as a play but of the pretense of the other plays produced along with it. As the play begins, it literally tears down the flats and machinery of the play which preceded it. As for itself, it is apologetic. The character Blue Jeans, who introduces it and is, in a sense, the major-domo of the play, is not a self-assured actor—he is not an actor at all, but a bashful, stumbling underling of the theater. Timidly he wishes to communicate a special emotion he feels and a special vision he sees. Consistently, his two characters are insignificant like himself.

The play is the lunch hour of two construction workers. The Old Man has led a life which we may guess has been unsuccessful in a material sense—in old age he is still a manual laborer. The Young Man can see perhaps little more than such a menial life ahead of him. Both characters possess a measure of pride, and they are both great pretenders because of this pride, though in different ways. The Young Man disclaims any part of the world he is in; his pseudo-anger comes from this disclaimer. The Old Man, on the other hand, has learned to glorify his life out of insignificance, through his imagination, and so to reconcile himself with his life.

The major technique of the play, seemingly to create itself out of nothing, acts as a metaphor of the Old Man's imaginative process. The Old Man becomes a teacher and the Young Man, in spite of himself, a willing student of this art of imaginative reconciliation. Blue Jeans sympathizes with his characters and helps them with their illusions. The lunch hour becomes a feast indeed. Yet, the play leaves with a trembling, perhaps tragic, realization: surely there is strength in the Old Man to accept the joy of the Feast as untarnished by the fact that it springs only from desire and illusion.

CHARACTERS

BLUE JEANS
OLD MAN
ANGRY YOUNG MAN
ELF WITH CHAMPAGNE (Blue Jeans disguised)
DROWSY CELLIST (likewise)

The curtains open . . . and . . . it must be some kind of mistake. The stage crew is still putting up sets. But no one seems to be much bothered by the fact. It might be a nice touch, though, to have a director, troubled species, to look up and notice. He might shout some muffled expletive off stage about who was the fool who opened the curtains etc., when they weren't ready. But in any case, the stage work-lights remain on, the stage work continues, somebody's complaining about a costume that doesn't fit, and damnitall if the curtains don't stay open. Now some character in blue jeans and spotted shirt comes out along the front of the stage. He is carrying an easel over his shoulder, a large piece of cardboard in his hand, and a pot of paint. For the sake of somebody's reputation, he might smile an apology to the audience. At any rate, when he gets to the opposite end of the stage, he sets up his easel, places the cardboard upon it facing the audience, and paints—rather scrawls, "THE FEAST." He puts his pot of paint aside and sits down on the stage next to his easel. He looks out at the audience and, twirling his glasses in his hand, begins:

BLUE JEANS. Well, now . . . no one said it was going to be an extraordinary sort of play . . . I mean, as a matter of fact, it's quite an ordinary sort of . . . Believe me, it doesn't deserve much of . . . You know, come to think of it, it's such an ordinary . . . I mean, I, for one, wouldn't feel so bad about dispensing with . . . uh . . . that is, I don't want to bother them for the sake of the feast. After all, you start stomping around on the grounds of every whim and . . . well, people get mad. So, we'll just let them go on working . . . go on, go right on and . . . then we can maybe sneak in this bit . . . (*He saunters back among the stagemen and, in a pantomime, wangles two tin buckets, which he brings forward, arranging them about five feet apart.*) . . . I've got friends . . . or, sometimes I seem to . . . CHARLIE (*Calls over audience.*) hey . . . HEY CHARLIE . . . (*A spot comes on, and* BLUE JEANS *waves it over to where he is standing between the buckets. The stage work-lights remain on.* B.J. *places a can on top of one of the buckets.*) I've got characters too, or sometimes I seem . . . they are supposed to arrive . . . (*Factory whistle.* BLUE JEANS *holds up his hand to the audience, nods his head.*) . . . a whistle, if you hadn't guessed, and it signals the start of this play. It makes a suitable sound to start a play? . . . right? It blows, and people change . . . you know, it toots, and people are possessed by it. It beckons in the harbor, and people look up expectant. Maybe it calls from the factory stacks . . . feet move, sometimes a smile . . . and you know it's our own creation, but we pray in our exertion to . . . A CHERUB OUT THERE perhaps. He looks down and chuckles at our business, but he takes up his horn and sounds pause, "take pause" . . . (*The whistle blows again.* B.J. *is about ready to climb down in the orchestra—but one final word.*) . . . and so on, so forth. (*He makes himself comfortable in the first row.* OLD MAN *is heard humming outside.*)

OLD MAN (*enters through the audience down the center aisle. He is wearing spotted, baggy work pants supported from the shoulders of a red plaid wool shirt by suspenders. He is characterized by an ambling, joyful gait, and when he speaks, it is with the friendly, booming quality of a man who has found a sense of self-assurance and contentment. Go ahead and ham him up . . . no danger. You might as well. He walks all the way down the center aisle, swinging a lunch pail at his side, singing. He sings to the tune of "Freight train, freight train . . .".*). Lunch hour, lunch hour, goin' so faaaast . . . Lunch hour, lunch hour, goin' so faaast . . . Dum de dum, de dum de donn . . . so they won't know where I've gone . . . (*Climbs stage, eventually sees the tin can on the one bucket.*) . . . AH HA! Miserable tin can of a man that I am . . . counting the minutes till your lunch hour comes . . . (*Kicks the can off the bucket.*) TAKE THAT! . . . (OLD MAN *gazes after the can and chuckles contentedly.*)

> (*Several of the stage crew members are still working on the sets, but they are making less noise now. One of the crew calls "Lights!" off stage, and the stage work-lights go off. The red and white border lights remain on, along with the spot centered on the* OLD MAN *and on the two buckets . . .* OLD MAN *puts his lunch pail in front of him, and as he opens it,* ANGRY YOUNG MAN *enters from the side. He is wearing old pants and a denim jacket—on his head a battered tweed golf cap. He sits down on the second bucket and . . . facing the audience like the* OLD MAN, *explores the contents of his paper bag. During the conversation that follows,* OLD MAN *eats his lunch out of his lunch pail,* YOUNG MAN, *out of his paper sack.* OLD MAN *chews his lunch in delight.* YOUNG MAN *rips at his lunch in anger. They are about finished with lunch by the time the "feast" begins.* YOUNG MAN *is characterized by brooding, suspicious expressions of a rebelliousness which, I guess, he considers attractive. Certainly he holds no distinct notions of revolt, because you see, indications are that* YOUNG MAN *isn't all that bright. But anyway,* OLD MAN *hums;* YOUNG MAN *broods, and neither seems conscious of the other until* OLD MAN *glances over at* YOUNG MAN *and says offhandedly:*)

Ah, you are here too . . . So you have come to join in the Great, Green Lunch Hour—that moment of rapture and dizzy joy, that . . . uh, moment of freedom! and . . . (*No response from* ANGRY YOUNG MAN.) . . . so you have come too?

> YOUNG MAN (*glances around, realizes that* OLD MAN *has spoken to him*). Yeah, sure, I mean, what do you mean?

... of course I am here ... I mean I DON'T EVEN KNOW YOU, OLD MAN!

OLD MAN. As you wish ... was just trying to make conversation.

YOUNG MAN. Humph. (*Lights begin to fade.*)

OLD MAN. There's this little game, see, that I know ... makes new acquaintances come much easier ...

YOUNG MAN. Humph. (*Spot remains on.*)

OLD MAN. It starts out, you see, by me asking a question ... I ask you, "What did you have for breakfast this morning, stranger?"

YOUNG MAN. Yeah?

OLD MAN. Well, what did you have for breakfast this morning, stranger?

YOUNG MAN (*suspiciously*). Well, let me see now ... I had a big bowl of Sugar Crisp—yes, and a cup of coffee from the machine.

OLD MAN. Now I tell you what I had for breakfast. I had this magnificent combination of Wheat Chex ... I really like Wheat Chex ... and orange juice, sausage, eggs—poached with pepper—and toast with plenty of kumquat jam ...

YOUNG MAN. Look here, what kind of a game is this?

OLD MAN. Why ... it's called the comparative breakfasts game.

YOUNG MAN (*throwing his hat to the floor*). LOOK HERE, OLD MAN ... WHAT DIFFERENCE DOES IT MAKE WHAT I HAD FOR BREAKFAST ANYWAY ... I mean, A MAN'S BREAKFAST IS HIS OWN BUSINESS ... (Y.M. *sputters, dusts off his hat and goes back to his lunch bag.*)

OLD MAN. Exactly ... you see, disclosing one's breakfast, a very intimate matter indeed, presumes acquaintance and avoids all sorts of embarrassment. Now if I were to tell you what I'm having for lunch ... for instance, I say, "Well, lemme see, I've got a boiled egg and a thermos of vegetable beef soup and ... a salomy 'n' lettuce on rye ... (*Gleefully exhibits the contents of his lunch pail.*)

YOUNG MAN. LOOK HERE . . . I don't happen to be interested in your breakfast, or your lunch, or even your fridgin' dinner, for that matter . . .

(*Long pause.*)

OLD MAN. It's such a pleasant day out. I just thought maybe . . .

YOUNG MAN. Hey, Dad . . . So happens I think it's a lousy rotten day, and so happens I don't like eating lunch out here in this lousy, rotten storage lot . . . out of a lousy, rotten paper bag. So happens it's a grubby, lousy city in a grubby, rotten world filled up with a lotta grubby, lousy, rotten people . . . try that out for size on the old wazoo.

(OLD MAN *takes a crunchy bite from an apple.*)

OLD MAN. Why, I'd say you are bitter . . . you are bitter, aren't you?

YOUNG MAN. Yeah . . . I am . . . I'm real bitter (*Throws hat on floor again.*) WHAT'YA MEAN BITTER, ANYWAY? . . . WHAT KIND OF QUESTION'S *THAT*? AND WHAT IF I AM . . . (*Turns his back on* O.M., *who shrugs his shoulder. They go back to their lunch.*)

OLD MAN. Well . . . I was just interested, you know . . . I mean bitter people don't usually . . . don't come here, that is . . .

YOUNG MAN (*challenged*). What do you mean?

OLD MAN. But . . . come to the feast, of course.

YOUNG MAN. The WHAT?

OLD MAN. . . . the feast . . .

YOUNG MAN. Oh, "the feast" . . . look, if that's some underhanded way of telling me you don't like my company, it don't wash, see Dad . . . I've got as much right to this crummy can as the next Joe . . . and so maybe you don't like me, well that's just tough potatoes.

OLD MAN. Oh, you can do what you like . . . the feast is quite open, you know . . . I don't mean to say you weren't invited, in fact this very moment I ask you to be my special guest.

YOUNG MAN. Guest?

OLD MAN. Yes, at the feast.

YOUNG MAN. Yeah, sure, what feast?

OLD MAN. Right now . . . here.

YOUNG MAN. What the fat kind of a feast you expect to have out in this crummy lot . . . I know about feasts, you think I'm dumb or something? . . . You think I'm dumb? My old lady used to tell me about feasts. She used to work at the Regis, and she used to bring junk back to the place and tell me about all the food and the people getting potted and dancing and smoking big cigars.

OLD MAN. Well, you see, this feast is a little different. I mean, your mother . . .

YOUNG MAN. You can leave her out of this. What gives you the right to sit there and . . .

OLD MAN. Really, I'm sure your mother is a very fine woman. I just want to explain . . .

YOUNG MAN. Well, for your information, so happens the old lady can take it in the ear for all I'm concerned.

(*Long pause.*)

OLD MAN. Let me explain about the feast.

YOUNG MAN. OK, OK, I'm willing to go along with a gag . . . the feast . . . shoot.

OLD MAN. Well take, for example, that little fellow over there on the corner playing the flute.

YOUNG MAN. Where . . . you mean that corner?

OLD MAN. Yes, over there . . . the little fellow with the flute.

YOUNG MAN. Oh, yeah. You mean the traffic cop—sure, I see the traffic cop.

OLD MAN. NO! NO! Not the traffic cop . . . "traffic cop" . . . the little fellow on the corner with a red bandana on his head playing the *flute!*

YOUNG MAN. The newsboy . . . maybe?

OLD MAN. NO! Not the newsboy . . . you mean to say you don't see a little man wearing a green coat and a red bandana, dancing around the bus stop sign, playing a flute? (*He makes a motion as if playing a flute.*)

YOUNG MAN. LOOK! I don't see any little guy in a green coat and a red bandana dancing around any bus stop sign, playing any fridgin' flute on THAT CORNER!

OLD MAN. Well, I suppose that's understandable.

YOUNG MAN. OK. What's the catch?

OLD MAN. My fine young man, any fool, if he uses his eyes, can plainly see that there is no little man with a flute and a bandana ... quite obviously, he is not there.

YOUNG MAN (*pause, nods his head, barely restraining his impulse to throw his hat on the floor*). Yes, I ... I see ... yes, that ... come to think of it ... that's surely the reason why I couldn't see the guy with the flute.

OLD MAN. Now, the feast is about the same as the little man with the flute, you know.

YOUNG MAN. Yeah, I get it, you mean I'm not going to be able to see the feast either ... well, you didn't have to tell me that!

OLD MAN. NO, NO ... not in the least ... you see the feast is like the little man because it is not ... for the most part, essentially and in *factum* ... there.

YOUNG MAN. Yeah, sure ... but, uh ... how we going to have the feast if it is not there? ... or here?

OLD MAN. Ah ... no more time to explain ... the feast is about to begin. But there's one small matter to settle first.

YOUNG MAN. And what's that?

OLD MAN. Why, the sort of feast that you prefer, of course.

YOUNG MAN. Now, don't tell me we have a choice even ... of feasts, that is.

OLD MAN. Absolutely! You have the broadest choice of all the choices, so you just say which it is that you prefer, and we will see what we can do.

YOUNG MAN. Yes, well ... I'm not exactly up on this feast jazz. What sort of choices do I have?

OLD MAN. GREAT SCOTT! Let's see ... you have wedding feasts, birthday feasts, feasts for coronation celebrations, vengeance feasts, mercy feasts and ... funeral feasts, war feasts, peace feasts ... whether you win or lose, you always have a feast ... and you have feasts for kings, feasts for thieves, demagogues, churchmen, salesmen, boatmen, law men, small men ... let's see, there are New Year feasts, Easter feasts, Christmas, Halloween, Arbor Day, Ground Hog's Day ...

YOUNG MAN. Yes, but there's really no fridgin' reason to have a feast, come right down to it.

OLD MAN. I was hoping you'd say that, because you see, that's the best sort of feast to have.

YOUNG MAN. Sure ... what's that?

OLD MAN. Why, the feast for no fridgin' ... er, Phrygian reason, as you put it.

YOUNG MAN. Yeah, sure ... that's bound to be the best ... uh, feast.

OLD MAN. Certainly the best ... no red tape of emotion to tangle up the revelry, no sticky cause, you see ... no cloud of duty hanging overhead ... yes, the feast for feast's sake is, without a doubt, the best.

YOUNG MAN. Anything you say, Dad ... it's your show, but seriously, how're you going to have any kind of a feast when all you've got left is half a salomy 'n' lettuce, and me ... (*Holding up his sandwich fragment.*) ...

OLD MAN. Come, lad ... the feast is not essentially a matter for eating. Food is but a key to the door where most any key will fit, you see ... It is that moment when the appetite is satisfied, when hunger is bubbled away (*Slaps his stomach.*), and the door opens on the magical land-scape of the FEAST! (OLD MAN *strikes a dramatic pose and slowly lifts his hands to the ceiling.* YOUNG MAN *sits awed at the* OLD MAN'*s invocation. The spotlight is by now the only light on the stage.*) OH, BACCHUS! SPIRIT OF MIRTH! SPIRIT OF SONG! LOOK DOWN WITH FAVOR UPON US ... SMILE THE SMILE OF MER-RIMENT, for why have we come but for the sake of mer-riment? Do we come to honor the living or the dead? Do we come to goad ourselves to victory or to cheer the vic-tory already won? NO! Do we come in the guise of char-ity and pity? Or do we come in the guise of business and serious matters? NO! NONE OF THESE! WE HAVE COME TO THIS GRAND FEAST FOR NO FRIDG-ING ... er, PHRYGIAN REASON AT ALL! ... so to speak—but for the sake of merriment. Let us, oh Bacchus, celebrate this moment!

YOUNG MAN (*whispering to* OLD MAN). Hey, cut it out! You want somebody to see us and think we're nuts? You want to be shipped off to the booby hatch or something?

OLD MAN. . . . I look upon the vaulted hall, the ranks of bountiful tables smiling in their candlelight. I see kindred faces, expectant faces . . . How best to celebrate this occasion which is, of course, no occasion, we ask. I present to you our special guest (OLD MAN *waves an arm in* YOUNG MAN's *direction.* YOUNG MAN *shrinks back.*) Here is a mind of vigor and youth. He represents a promise for our age . . .

YOUNG MAN (*whispering*). *Look here, Old Man,* I don't know what you're up to, but I sure as fat don't like it. I didn't ask to get into this. I . . . I was sucked into this flaming feast, you know damn well I was . . . come on now.

OLD MAN. Ladies and gentlemen, I present to you a young man with depth of spirit, breadth of heart, and fullness of imagination . . .

YOUNG MAN (*still whispering*). This is no fair, you tricked me . . . you trapped me . . . you . . . (*Shouts in* OLD MAN's *ear.*) . . . FRUITCAKE! (OLD MAN *not fazed.* YOUNG MAN *hastily stoops to pick up his bag and lunch papers, puts on his cap in preparation for flight.*)

OLD MAN. . . . in short, I present to you the Angry Young Man. (OLD MAN *catches* YOUNG MAN *by the sleeve and leads him into the spotlight.*)

YOUNG MAN. Look here, this gag of yours has gone far enough . . . go right ahead and spout off if you want, just leave me out of it . . . uh, just feast it by yourself, why don't you?

OLD MAN (*whispering*). Don't spoil it all . . . this is part of the bit. There always has to be some sort of a keynote speech at every feast.

YOUNG MAN. But really, Dad. This is ridiculous . . . I mean, really.

OLD MAN. I don't know what you're so worried about. All you have to do is to say a few words to them . . .

YOUNG MAN. To WHO?

OLD MAN. To them ... (*Indicates the audience.*) It's just part of the bit, you know.

YOUNG MAN. OK, OK. Nobody's going to say I'm not a good sport, a good Joe, an allright guy ... just so long as you agree that if someone happens to come by, it's all a joke, see ... Let's make this short ... what am I supposed to say?

OLD MAN. Well, let me see ... you ought to say something about the reason for the feast which, of course, will be a hard part ... you just say what you like. Yes, and add something about how distinguished the audience is ... appeal to the emotions, their pity, amuse them, flatter them, agree with them ...

YOUNG MAN. OK, anything you say. Remember, I'm just going along with the gag. (*Takes off his hat and faces the audience with an embarrassed smile, then turns towards the* OLD MAN *again.*) Aw, come on. This is crazy.

OLD MAN (*whispering*). Go on, go on ...

YOUNG MAN (*turns to the audience, smiling again*). Ladies and gentlemen ... I'm not much on speeches really ... (*Turns.*) How's that?

OLD MAN. Fine, fine. Their sympathy is already with you.

YOUNG MAN (*facing the audience again*). .... and believe me, it's like a great honor to be here at this moment before you. Now let me tell you about a funny thing that happened to me during my lunch hour. I was sitting there, see, and this old geezer invites me to this feast, just for a gag (*Glances at* OLD MAN.) and so ... uh, here I am. And the introduction that the Old Man gave me was way out ... I mean it was too much. But, consider the reason why we are all here ... What is the reason we're all here, after all? ... Damned if I know. Man, the whole thing is really ... uh, crazy. (*Glances at* OLD MAN.) Well, there doesn't seem to be any reason for being here—how about all the reasons for not being here? Just put that in your pipe and smoke it. Just think of all the things you might be doing instead of wasting your time at this, uh ... feast.

You could be putting the garbage out. You could be running over rabbits in your car (*Whispers* "Pity" *to* OLD MAN, *who nods his head in approval.*) ... you could be shoplifting in a super-market or thinking up nasty comments to make to your mother-in-law. Just THINK of all the temptations you might be yielding to if you weren't wasting your time here, feasting it up ... It's great to have you here and ... So go right ahead and feast it up because it's great to be here (*Glances at* OLD MAN *for approval.*) and besides that, you are all really great people, and I really agree with you about everything ... thank you. (*Turns to* OLD MAN.) How was that?

OLD MAN. That was great, just great ... but wait, you may be called on to make a few toasts.

YOUNG MAN (*brow-beaten and confused*). Just give the word, Dad ... I can't make any more a fool of myself. (*He sits down, shaking his head.*)

OLD MAN. We thank the Angry Young Man for his remarks, always apt, well-chosen, short, and to the point. But the time for invocation has passed; the moment of preparation is accomplished ... Therefore, GIVE US WINE! Let us lift up our glasses and so lift up our hearts. (OLD MAN *looks down at the front row seat where* BLUE JEANS *is sitting.*) PSSSSST! That's your cue ... the wine ... (BLUE JEANS *gets up from his seat, goes back up the ladder, and is to be seen at one end of the stage, putting on a short green coat and wrapping a red bandana around his head, both of which were handed out to him from the wings.*)

YOUNG MAN. Wine?

OLD MAN. Of course. How can you drink a toast without wine?

YOUNG MAN. Yeah, sure. This I gotta see. (*Follows* BLUE JEANS *off stage in amazement.*)

OLD MAN. ... Bring flushes to our cheeks and so flush the general spirit with unencumbered mirth. (*A cart is pushed out onto the stage, and* BLUE JEANS *trundles it out towards the spotlight. The cart holds a bucket of ice with a bottle of champagne and several glasses.*) Sniff gently the wine's bouquet and rejoice in its sweet vapor. Smile, laugh ... feel warmth. (ELF *with champagne, i.e.,* BLUE JEANS, *rolls the cart into the spotlight.* YOUNG MAN *stares at him wide-eyed.* BLUE JEANS *answers the stare with an embarrassed shrug.* B.J. *pours out two glasses and hands one to* OLD MAN, *one to* YOUNG MAN.) I PROPOSE A TOAST ... (*Lifts up his glass*) ... TO THE FEAST ... THE FEAST FOR NO FRIDGIN' ... PHRYGIAN REASON, so the expression goes. (*Drinks, motioning to* YOUNG MAN *to do the same.*)

YOUNG MAN (*after lowering his glass*). This is ridiculous ...

OLD MAN. TO THE RIDICULOUS, THEN! (*They drink.*)

YOUNG MAN. This is UNREAL!

OLD MAN. TO THE UNREAL, IF YOU LIKE! (*They drink again.*)

YOUNG MAN. But I mean ... really ...

OLD MAN. DRINK! (*Drinks again. As* BLUE JEANS *refills the glasses,* OLD MAN *whispers to* YOUNG MAN.) Now it's your turn to make the toast ... (YOUNG MAN *hesitates.*) Go on, go on.

YOUNG MAN. Well, OK ... I propose a toast to, uh ...

OLD MAN. WHY NOT?!

YOUNG MAN (*slumping down on the bucket*). This is too much ... (BLUE JEANS *has been sneaking a few drinks himself.*)

OLD MAN. All right, all right. So much for the toasts. (*Smacks his lips.*) Let's on to the reading of the ode.

YOUNG MAN. Yeah, sure, "The Ode"!

OLD MAN. Any kind of feast that's worth its salt has a reading of a commemorative ode ... (*Takes a piece of paper from his shirt pocket and unfolds it.*) ... You don't want to read the ode, do you? Some people say the special guest should always read the ode.

YOUNG MAN. Oh, no ... uh, you just go right ahead, and I'll just sort of sit here and listen.

OLD MAN. As you prefer. (*During this time,* BLUE JEANS *has taken off his green coat and bandana, handing them*

*off stage. He runs to the other side of the stage and slips
into a tails coat and buttons on a white tie. He carries a
cello and a small stool out to the edge of the spotlight, sits
down and prepares to play. He yawns and stretches, waiting for* OLD MAN *to begin the reading of the ode.*) I
present to you the ODE, forever commemorating this feast
... our feast without reason or occasion.

> (OLD MAN *motions for the* CELLIST *to begin his back-
> ground music, waits a moment, then sighing, begins.
> As the ode progresses,* CELLIST *falls almost asleep,
> bowing of cello is spasmodic, but recorded music
> plays on.*)

OLD MAN'S ODE

Oh Bacchus, look this way!
See the anger mapping lines upon our brow, trace the print
of trouble's foot around our eyes—
Dismal creatures we must seem, cowering behind the day's
affairs,
Grasping tight to tin toy soldiers of our objective lives,
staring, as imagination dies;
See our mental siege and send down laughing legions to set
us free.

Thus did we call out to Bacchus, and he raised a drunken
eyebrow to our plea.
He sent to us, not legions, but a Cherub from his troop,
One small, fat, sodden Cherub (*Looks at* BLUE JEANS.)
from his troop.

Oh Cherub, harken to our woe!
Listen, minor spirit of the feast, fledgling sent by Bacchus
giving answer to our plea,
Thou, who now would far rather be thronged among thy
master's ranks,
Voicing his choral praise, or tipping the Olympian cup
upon your lip to drain his liquid revelry,

Listen to our labor's chant, and grant, at least, a momentary feast!

Thus, did we call out to the Cherub Bacchus sent, still pouting from his journey,

He blinked his eyes, and then his pudgy mouth gaped open in a yawn,

But he gave us music, and he gave us wine before our time was up.

(*Factory whistle blows. All characters look up. The lights begin to fade on again.* BLUE JEANS *takes his cello and stool off stage, along with his costume. He comes back out and grabs the glasses away from* YOUNG MAN, *who resists, and from* OLD MAN, *who is resigned.* BLUE JEANS *trundles the champagne cart off stage. The lights come up quickly now. The stage work-lights are flipped on. The stage crew members begin to return to their task of putting up sets.*)

YOUNG MAN (*looking around him, bewildered*). The wine . . . the guy with the . . . uh, violin? Where have they gone? The feast. . . what happened?

OLD MAN. Time was up, that's all.

YOUNG MAN. What do you mean, the time was up . . . I mean they were all here . . . and your ode? Where's your ode?

OLD MAN (*checking through his pockets*). I guess I lost it . . . (*He had set it down on the cart.*) . . . anyway, you heard the whistle, didn't you . . . back to work, you know. (*Cheerful.*)

YOUNG MAN. I guess so . . . (OLD MAN *climbs down the ladder after gathering up his things.* YOUNG MAN *puts his lunch papers in the paper bag and crumples it up. He gazes up the aisle as* OLD MAN *leaves.*)

OLD MAN (*turns somewhere up the aisle*). So long, Young Man . . .

YOUNG MAN. So long, Old Man . . . (*Turns and walks slowly off stage pondering something. As he goes,* BLUE JEANS *bustles out from the wings, gathers up his easel and*

cardboard and ladder. In his rush he bumps into YOUNG
MAN, *says,* "Excuse me . . .". YOUNG MAN *barely notices.*)
    (BLUE JEANS *bustles off the other side of the stage;
    someone among the stage crew looks up, and noticing
    that some damn fool has opened the curtain when
    they weren't ready, shouts some expletive off stage.*)
    (*The curtains close hurriedly.*)

WAITING
FOR THE
BUS

❧

by Ramon Delgado

Author's Note

Waiting for the Bus is an allegorical, theatrical poem, which depicts the progress of Western man and his prospects for the future. Edith represents the life force, the eternal mother, the protector and defender of the home, the family, and the society. Andrew represents the civilized man of cultural accomplishments whose vision has become blurred through lack of faith in the intangibles of life. The bus, which runs over Andrew, demonstrates the power of Edith's vision over Andrew's. Edith has played the game so well that her wishes have become reality.

Benny and Cynthia each represent a prejudice in the minds of the main characters. Benny, of course, is the object of Andrew's racial prejudice, and Cynthia is the object of Edith's social prejudice. These elements prevent Andrew and Edith from seeing life without astigmatism.

Even though Edith's viewpoint prevails over Andrew's, she is lost without Andrew, and her pleas for someone to fill his position can be answered only by the lower animals. Edith wins the game, only to lose the partner that made it meaningful. Unwilling or unable to perceive the nothingness beneath the game, Edith played to win, and so came to believe the game as reality itself. The story reaches a resting point with the death of Andrew, but the dilemma remains: Is it better to live aware of the games one plays in life convinced that there is nothing beneath them; or is it better to accept the games as the only reality, deluding oneself with false hope?

The form of the play was influenced by *The Chairs,* a one-act by Eugene Ionesco, but the main characters, though perhaps reminiscent of the elderly couple in Ionesco's play, actually sprang from a trio of senior citizens who performed many of the incidents in the play in their own lives. Another less obvious literary influence on the play is Thornton Wilder's *The Skin of Our Teeth.* Andrew, Edith, and Cynthia are in many ways a Mr. and Mrs. Antrobus and Sabina grown older but not wiser.

CHARACTERS

EDITH (an old, old woman, the man's wife)
ANDREW (an old, old man, the woman's husband)
CYNTHIA (an old woman—of ill repute)
BENNY (a black shoeshine boy)
FEATHERS (an invisible parakeet)
TOTO (an invisible dog)

The scene is the city park. A bench L.C. faces the audience. A mail box stands in the D.R. corner; a street lamp R.C. A zoo is not so far away, and the sounds of the animals can be heard, dimly, but distinctly.

The stage is empty at the rise of the curtain, but shortly, EDITH *and* ANDREW *hobble in D.R., each trying to support the other, each failing miserably, because at the same time they are rolling a baby buggy with a bird cage in it and pulling on a leash attached to an imaginary dog.*

Acting note: A presentational approach to the characters may help the actors achieve the style of the play more fully than a representational approach.

EDITH. The blind leading the blind—and when the blind lead the blind, they shall both fall in a ditch. You really ought to get your glasses changed, Andrew.

ANDREW. I can see well enough, my dear.

(ANDREW *stops R.C. a moment and begins wiping his shoes on the grass.*)

EDITH. What's the matter, Andrew?

ANDREW. Damn dogs, dumb animals, you can't educate them!

EDITH. You shouldn't curse, my **love**, besides it isn't the dog's fault. It's your eyes. They're getting weaker, and you must take care of your eyes, they're the only ones you'll ever have.

ANDREW. Now, Edith, at my age new glasses are hardly worth the expense. And don't let the dogs get out of this either. They know where the grass is, and they can tell the difference between grass and sidewalk, but leave it to you to defend the dumbest animals.

EDITH. Wasn't that a lovely zoo we just passed, Andrew?

ANDREW. The animals smelled.

EDITH. Of course animals smell—that's part of being alive.

ANDREW. Not smell then—stink. The animals stink—stinked? Stunk? Anyway, there were musky odors, and rancid odors and rotten odors and moldy odors and reeking odors and effluvious odors and—

EDITH. Andrew, you must admit the animals have helped us many times.

ANDREW (*crossing to L. end of bench*). Well, we have machines to do everything now.

EDITH (*crossing to R. end of bench*). But we must be grateful to them for the dog sled, the mule team, the ox cart, the reindeer sled, the camel caravan, the ostrich buggy, the peace doves, and you must admit some of them are smart—trained seals, educated elephants, performing lions and tigers, dancing zebras, movie star porpoises, wrestling bears, fighting roosters, talking dogs, verbose parrots—

ANDREW. If they're so intelligent, then why haven't they shown more cooperation in the efforts for peace?

EDITH. Why, Andrew, didn't I tell you? Our little Toto, our own little snoopy dog, has learned to sit up on his hind paws and lift his front legs and beg.

ANDREW. That I can believe.

EDITH (*sitting on R. end of bench*). Now you just watch. Come here, Toto. That's a nice little puppy. Now —sit. That's it—Now show Daddy what you can do.

ANDREW. Don't call me his daddy.

EDITH. Oh, Andrew, you've insulted Toto. Now he won't perform.

ANDREW. Just like an actor.

EDITH (*placing the bird cage on the bench between them*). Maybe Feathers will say a few of the words she has learned—Now don't insult her, too, Andrew.

ANDREW. I won't say it, but I'll think it.

EDITH. Think what, dear?

ANDREW. That Feathers isn't worth her parakeet seed.

EDITH. Now you've gone and done it. She's put her head under her wing. She loves to show off for friendly people. Look what you've done to her, Andrew. You've made an introvert of her.

ANDREW. My humble apologies.

EDITH. And just when she was getting along so nicely. She's getting much plainer, too. Why only yesterday she said—

ANDREW (*sitting L. end of bench*). I'm not interested.

EDITH. But, Andrew, children must be loved.

ANDREW. But Toto and Feathers are not our children, besides we're at the bus station, and I don't want the people to stare.

EDITH. When our other children left home, you said we would take care of Toto and Feathers, and they could go everywhere we went.

ANDREW. I didn't say I'd adopt them.

EDITH. Two more wouldn't hurt. We've only had twenty-seven billion, six hundred and fifty-four million, three hundred and eighty-one thousand, one hundred and two. Two more won't make much difference.

ANDREW. I absolutely refuse to adopt them.

EDITH. You will take them on the bus though, won't you, Andrew?

ANDREW. They'll have to ride in the luggage compartment.

EDITH. They'll smother to death.

ANDREW. They can't sit in the seats with us. What will the bus driver say? And you're sure to poke someone in the eye with that bird cage.

EDITH. Well, you ask the ticket man if they can't go. He'll tell you.

ANDREW. However, if they do go, it would make a good anecdote for my memoirs.

EDITH. Ah, yes, your memoirs. Do let them go, Andrew.

ANDREW. Only if the ticket man and the bus driver

agree, which is highly unlikely for any two men in such administrative positions.

EDITH. Maybe you could start writing your memoirs on the trip.

ANDREW. Bad roads.

EDITH. But if you don't start now, you may never finish.

ANDREW. I shall not start my memoirs until I am no longer able to travel, but in the mean time I shall continue to keep little notes of all the things that have happened to us.

EDITH. Your library is full of notebooks. What was the last count?

ANDREW (*standing*). Let me see, what did I do with that piece of paper? (*He takes out an imaginary bit of paper.*) I counted last week, and wrote it down. (*Behind L. end of bench.*) Here it is—seventy-five billion, six hundred and thirty-nine million, eight hundred and twenty-three thousand, nine hundred and ninety-nine. And with the notes I shall make on this trip, we may pass the seventy-six billion mark.

EDITH. My, my, all those notes. And how many volumes of memoirs will that make?

ANDREW. Well, when I subtract the duplication of events, the unimportant incidents, the adventures we started and never finished, the inventions that were failures, the languages that are dead, the characters who are only names, it should come roughly to one small volume.

EDITH. I can hardly wait to get back and help you begin your organization.

ANDREW (*crossing behind* EDITH, *pats her on the shoulder*). You have always been a faithful secretary.

EDITH. If I can't help you, Andrew, I would die. We have enjoyed life together, haven't we?

ANDREW. Yes, we have enjoyed life more than the average, I would say.

EDITH. We have many more years together, don't you think, Andrew?

ANDREW (*a distant echo*). Many more years.

EDITH. I hope we don't die separately. I hope we are killed together in a bus accident.

ANDREW (*a distant echo*). Together in a bus accident.

EDITH. Maybe it will be this time—but I hope not because you haven't written your memoirs. Where are we going today, Andrew?

ANDREW. The scenic route.

EDITH. I always enjoy the scenic routes. The long trip or the short one.

ANDREW (*R. end of bench*). The short one. We must hurry back, you know.

EDITH. Yes, so you'll have plenty of time to write.

ANDREW (*in the manner of a train announcer*). We're going to Charleston, Charlotte, Roanoke, Richmond, Washington, Newark, Boston, Ottawa, Winnipeg, Nome, Vladivostok, Yokohama, Sydney, Shanghai, Calcutta, Nazareth, Alexandria, Cologne, Heidelberg, Liverpool, Dublin, Johannesburg, Santiago, Rio de Janeiro, San Jose, Havana, Miami, and Atlantis.

EDITH. My, my. That is the short trip. Now, when you buy the tickets tell the ticket seller that you were once a general.

ANDREW. What for?

EDITH. That should impress him and make him give you the best seats on the bus.

ANDREW. I don't see what difference that would make.

EDITH. Oh, the prestige that goes with being a general! He will know that you should have been president, because everybody knows that generals make the best presidents.

ANDREW. I just wasn't popular enough.

EDITH. I was proud of you, dear. Even when you lost. But tell the ticket man what battles you were in. Tell him how well you fought, for, dear, that is the one thing you really do well, in fact, I would say you do that best of all.

ANDREW. Except my memoirs.

EDITH. Yes, your memoirs—they shall be even greater than your battles.

ANDREW. They were so long ago, and now I have only their memory—I am past fighting, past desire.

EDITH (*a distant echo*). Past, past desire.

ANDREW. Past hope.

EDITH (*a distant echo*). Past, past hope. (*Scolding.*) Andrew, don't say that!

ANDREW. It's true, dear. We're on our way downhill. We have just passed middle age only last year. Past hope, past desire.

EDITH. Nonsense, now you go get the tickets, and I'll wait right here for you. Go along now.

ANDREW. All right, but my heart isn't in it anymore. I do this just to keep my mind occupied. I'm too old for pretend.

EDITH. We're not old yet. Now do as I say.

ANDREW. You always take our games too seriously anyway.

EDITH. Well, a body's got to take something in life seriously, or he'd soon go crazy. Now run along with you.

ANDREW. All right, my dear, I'll keep up the game. As long as you can keep up your end, I'll keep up mine.

EDITH. Hurry along. We'll miss the bus. If we don't have our tickets, the bus will go right along without us.

(ANDREW *crosses to the mail box D.R., but on the way he bumps into the lamp post.*)

ANDREW. Pardon me, miss. I thought you were a lamp post.

EDITH. Andrew, you do need your glasses changed. Something dreadful is going to happen to you if you don't.

ANDREW. Dreadful if I don't.

(ANDREW *gets to the mail box, and pantomimes a conversation with the invisible ticket man; he looks back at* EDITH *every once in a while; she smiles reassuringly. He continues.* EDITH *talks to* TOTO *and* FEATHERS.)

EDITH. Toto, you should be ashamed of yourself. After all the care we've given you. I know Andrew gets irritated every once in a while, but you could make him smile by doing your cute tricks. And Feathers, I can't imagine what has gotten into you. You were so chipper this morning when we started out. Now, don't you worry. I'm going to see that you get to go on the trip this time.

(ANDREW *returns and sits on L. end of bench.*)
Well, what did he say? Did you get the tickets?

ANDREW. Left coat pocket.

EDITH. And the animals, can they go?

ANDREW. He said the only way the animals could go was for the bus driver to say okay.

EDITH. Did you tell the man about your being a general and all that?

ANDREW. I told him everything.

EDITH. What did he say?

ANDREW. He said the bus would be late.

EDITH. It always is.

ANDREW. All we can do is wait.

EDITH. We must play a game to pass the time. What shall we play, Andrew? You're good at games.

ANDREW. A game within a game.

EDITH. I don't understand, Andrew.

ANDREW. Nothing. It doesn't matter. What game do you want to play?

EDITH. Let's play—chase.

ANDREW. Too strenuous.

EDITH. Let's play—making wishes.

ANDREW. Too tame.

(*Pause.*)

EDITH (*as if reading something in front of her*). Nickels, quarters, dimes.

ANDREW. What's that?

EDITH. I say nickels, quarters, dimes.

ANDREW. Well, what are you saying it for? Is that the name of a new game?

EDITH. No, I was just reading the instructions on the cigarette machine. Nickels, quarters, and dimes only. But of course that isn't true, is it?

ANDREW. Of course not.

EDITH. Because there are also annas, centavos, pesos, lire, francs, sous, drachmas, kopeks, reis, sen, yen, farthings, florins, salt, whiskey, wampum, ginger, and mites.

ANDREW. In God We Trust!

(*Another pause.*)

EDITH (*as if reading something in front of her*). Mild, very mild.

ANDREW. What's that.

EDITH. I say mild, very mild. The sign on the cigar box. You should never have given up smoking, Andrew.

ANDREW. Why not?

EDITH. You could blow the most perfect smoke rings.

ANDREW. Any circle is perfect.

EDITH. Oh, let's not bother about geometry today, or any other of the mathematics. I'm tired of figures. Let's think about words instead. (*Rises, crosses behind* AN-DREW.) That's a wonderful idea, Andrew. We can pass the time by making up words.

ANDREW. You just don't make up words by thinking about it.

EDITH (*over his shoulders*). Why not? You've made up millions.

ANDREW. But only when the occasion arose that needed a new word.

EDITH. Have you ever seen those trees look just exactly like they look now?

ANDREW. No, not exactly, why?

EDITH. Well, then we need a word for it—frilting.

ANDREW. Frilting?

EDITH. Frilting! I frilt, you frilt, he, she, or it frilts. The trees are frilting.

ANDREW. And exactly what does that mean?

EDITH. It means exactly what the trees are doing right now—nothing more, nothing less. Goodness, if I could tell you what a word meant by using another word, there wouldn't be much use in having new words at all, would there?

ANDREW. I guess not, but how are you going to explain to someone else what you mean?

EDITH. Nothing simpler. Just bring the people here and show them the trees. You point to the trees and you say "frilting." It's really a very nice word—and more fun to say than eating a chocolate covered cherry. Come on, try it.

ANDREW. This is ridiculous!

EDITH. Try it. For me, Andrew.

ANDREW. Oh, all right. Frilting! Frilting! Frilting! Say, you're right.

EDITH. Strench!

ANDREW. How's that!

EDITH. Strench. That's what you experienced when we passed by the zoo—a strong stench—strench—oh, Andrew, this is fun. I don't know why we didn't start this game a long time ago.

ANDREW. If we had, the language would be cluttered up with thousands of useless words.

EDITH. Oh, you're just against progress. Besides it passes the time.

ANDREW. Sitting and meditating passes the time, too.

(ANDREW *looks at* EDITH *sharply. She sits on R. end of bench.*)

(*Pause.*)

EDITH. Oh, Andrew, I almost forgot to mail the letter to our last child, telling him where we're going.

ANDREW. The child won't care.

EDITH. What a thing to say! Our children always care.

ANDREW. They never write us back.

EDITH. That doesn't mean they don't care. They have their own worries and responsibilities. Down in my heart, I know they still love us.

ANDREW. There's a mail box on the corner.

EDITH. I see it, dear, and *I* can even see it from here.

ANDREW. Well, go to it then.

EDITH (*rising*). Can I trust you with the animals?

ANDREW. Of course.

EDITH. They'd better be all right when I get back.

ANDREW. They'll be just as you left them.

EDITH (*putting bird cage in baby buggy*). Just the same I think I'll take Feathers with me.

(EDITH *crosses to the mail box, pushing the baby*

> *buggy with the bird cage in it. As she mails the im-*
> *aginary letter, she gets her hand stuck in the vent on*
> *the mail box.*)

Andrew, Andrew, help me.

ANDREW (*rising*). What's the matter, dear?

EDITH. My hand. The mail box. Stuck, dear.

(ANDREW *crosses to* EDITH's *L.*)

ANDREW. You should have let me mail the letter for you.

EDITH. You didn't offer to.

ANDREW. You should have asked me. I would have been happy to. There, is that better?

EDITH. Kiss it, and make it well.

(ANDREW *does.*)

Oh, Andrew, you have rescued me from danger so many times. You have saved me from the dragon, from the noose, from burning at the stake, from the guillotine, from the rack, from the famine, from the flood, from the cross, and from the lions. And now from the mail box! My, my, how brave you still are! And why did you do all this, Andrew?

ANDREW. Must I say? Don't you know?

EDITH. I never get tired of hearing you say it. You once had the voice of an orator, a politician, an opera baritone, an actor, a prince, and even now I can hear that voice. Tell me as you always tell me when you rescue me.

ANDREW. My dearest, I love you.

EDITH. And there has never been another?

ANDREW. Never.

EDITH. And there will never be another?

ANDREW. Never.

EDITH. How comforting to know that. For I am extremely jealous of you. You know that, don't you?

ANDREW. The people are staring, Edith.

EDITH. Let them stare. What do they know of our deep romance. I don't care if the world knows that you are my husband. I am proud to be your wife.

ANDREW. Past desire—past hope.

EDITH. Kiss me, Andrew.

ANDREW. Right here, in public?

EDITH. In the eyes of God!

ANDREW. On the mouth?

EDITH. On my trembling lips!

ANDREW. I can't. Not out in the open like this.

EDITH. Many other people do.

ANDREW. Well—I don't want to be too different from other people.

(ANDREW *kisses* EDITH.)

EDITH. Mild, very mild.

(BENNY, *the black shoeshine boy, enters D.L.*)
Oh, look, Andrew.

BENNY (*L.C.*). Shine, mister?

EDITH. Andrew, he's talking to you.

ANDREW. Sons of Ham, cursed by Noah, servants of Shem.

EDITH. He only wants to shine your shoes.

ANDREW (*crossing behind lamp post*). I don't want to have them shined.

EDITH (*crossing to* BENNY, *D.L.C.*). Why, Andrew, look at the child—I do believe he's one of ours.

ANDREW. Don't be unreasonable.

EDITH. Tell me, little boy, what's your name?

BENNY. I's named Benny, mam.

EDITH. Andrew, we had a Benny once. A-B-C-D—yes, right between Abel and Cain. Do you suppose it's the same one?

ANDREW. Sons of Ham, cursed by—

EDITH. Tell me, little boy, are we your parents?

BENNY. I don't know. I don't know what parents is.

EDITH. Poor little thing. He hasn't any parents. (*Crossing to* ANDREW'S *L.*) Andrew, we could adopt him. Make him our very own.

ANDREW. Servants of Shem.

EDITH. Now that's no way to talk. If the child is an orphan, the least we can do is be foster parents to him.

BENNY. Don't want no foster parents. I'm a shoeshine boy. Shoeshine boys shine shoes. They don't need no parents.

(BENNY *exits D.R.*)

EDITH (*crossing D.R.*). Wait, little boy.

ANDREW (*crossing to L. end of bench*). Let him go.

EDITH (*crossing to* ANDREW's *R.*). Andrew, you've no right to turn him away like that.

ANDREW. Sons of Ham, cursed by Noah, servants of Shem.

EDITH. Andrew, you must remember that even if he isn't our son, he's a close relative.

ANDREW. Over my dead body.

EDITH. Maybe you don't keep track of the family. But I do, and one way or another, we're all related. We're related by aunts and great-grandmothers and second cousins, and uncles and fourth cousins twice removed and great-great-great-grandaddies and marriages among families and marriages between families and marriages outside of families. You never know when you meet a person that he might not be closer related to you than your own children, and that's a fact.

ANDREW. I don't see it that way.

EDITH. The trouble with you is you just don't see well at all.

(ANDREW *starts out D.L.*)

And where are you going, may I ask?

ANDREW. The comfort station, if you have to know.

EDITH. I thought you'd been acting mighty fidgety. Well, go ahead, don't let me stop you.

ANDREW. All right, I will.

(ANDREW *exits D.L.*)

EDITH (*crossing D.R. to get baby carriage*). Come, my pretty Feathers. You mustn't shiver like that. It's not cold. (*Crossing to R. end of bench.*) In fact, it's a rather pleasant day. There, that's better. Now you look like my baby should—perk and lively. Are you going to talk for Mama? (*Sits, R. end of bench.*) Well, Toto, of course I love you, too. I love all of my children. Now, now, you mustn't mind what Andrew says. Andrew is just like a child, too, in so many ways. Of course he's done some very remarkable things, his inventions, his languages, his wars, his notes for his memoirs. Just wait until he gets his memoirs pub-

lished. Then you'll see it hasn't all been in vain. He's tired
now, and this last trip will be a great relaxation before the
grind of writing, so you mustn't be too upset if he seems
irritated. I love Andrew. I have always loved Andrew, and
I shall love him forever—if I last that long. What's that,
Feathers? Why, Feathers, how wonderful! It's clear. It's
distinct. You will say that for Andrew when he comes,
won't you? For my sake? And Toto, you're sitting up perfectly. Here's a milk bone. Mama bought it for you. That's
a fine boy, a fine boy. Mama is proud of you both. Why,
Feathers, how did you learn to say that? Will miracles
never cease? All by yourself? You picked it up? Wait till
Andrew hears—just wait till he hears.

(CYNTHIA *enters D.R., crosses to L. end of bench.*)
Oh, hello. How do you do.

CYNTHIA. Fine, sister. How about yourself.

EDITH. Rather well, thank you.

CYNTHIA (*sitting*). Mind if I sit down?

EDITH. Not a bit. Be careful of Toto.

CYNTHIA. Who?

EDITH. Our dog.

CYNTHIA. Where?

EDITH. Right here, on the end of the leash.

CYNTHIA (*uneasily*). Oh—sure. Pretty, ain't he?

EDITH. I don't know that you'd exactly call him pretty.
Unique would be more correct.

CYNTHIA. Yeah, that's what I mean—a pretty unique
dog. (*Pause.*) My name's Cynthia, what's yours?

EDITH. My name is Edith, and my husband's name is
Andrew.

CYNTHIA (*nostalgically*). I knew an Andrew once—in
Germany.

EDITH (*warily*). In Germany—you don't say. When was
that?

CYNTHIA. Near the close of the war.

EDITH. Which one? There have been so many through
Germany.

CYNTHIA. I don't guess it was the same Andrew.

EDITH. He's been a soldier a good long time.

CYNTHIA. Well, I've been going around from country to country for a good long time too.

EDITH. And from man to man?

CYNTHIA. What makes you say that?

EDITH. I know your type. I can tell by the thick make-up. I've never understood that. Why does a woman in your "profession" cover herself with such heavy paint?

CYNTHIA. We have to work past our prime.

EDITH. Was it my Andrew you knew in Germany?

CYNTHIA. How do I know whether it was your Andrew or not. Men come and men go; and they don't leave their calling cards. There are Andrews all over the world.

EDITH. Did he tell you that he loved you?

CYNTHIA. They all say that.

EDITH. All of them?

CYNTHIA (*wistfully*). They used to.

EDITH. My Andrew wouldn't. He wouldn't even look at you.

CYNTHIA. Lady, I'm not going to argue with you. I don't know your Andrew from Adam's house cat, and if I weren't so dog tired, I'd walk on to find another bench.

EDITH. You had been running, hadn't you?

CYNTHIA. I'm always running—from something or to something.

EDITH. You don't have to, you know. You could get married.

CYNTHIA. I'd rather run.

EDITH. On the average, marriage is good for people.

CYNTHIA. When you've seen as many unfaithful men as I have, you don't have much faith in marriage.

EDITH. But the family is the foundation of our society, and without marriage—

CYNTHIA. Look, lady, you ain't gonna reform me. I heard all the gospel I could stand in the last Graham crusade.

EDITH. Just the same—

(ANDREW *enters D.L., giggling to himself.*)

(EDITH *rises.*)

Andrew, I want you to tell this woman—(*Crosses to* AN-

DREW's R.) Andrew, what is the matter with you? Stop that silly giggling.

ANDREW. I've seen it—the writing on the wall.

EDITH. On the wall?

ANDREW. The verses and quotations, the scriptures and passages, the jokes and songs on the wall of the comfort station.

EDITH. Andrew, be serious. I want you to—

ANDREW. And I have made an important decision.

EDITH. Andrew, this woman—

ANDREW. And I am sure that history will prove that all important decisions were made by some great man sitting on the john.

EDITH. Andrew, that isn't very nice.

ANDREW. Hello—who is this?

EDITH. Her name is Cynthia. Will you please tell her to go away?

ANDREW (*crossing to* CYNTHIA's *L.*). No, indeed. Didn't you tell me we were all related? She may be my kissing cousin.

EDITH. Past desire, past hope?

ANDREW. Past desire, but not past hope.

EDITH. You mustn't even look at such a woman.

ANDREW (*crossing to R. end of bench*). It doesn't do any harm to look.

EDITH (*crossing to* CYNTHIA's *L. and tugging her up by her arm*). Run along, miss. Our bus will be here in just a little while.

CYNTHIA. I've got just as much right to be here as you have.

EDITH. We don't want you.

ANDREW (*crossing to* CYNTHIA's *R.*). Well, I want her. I want her to go on the bus trip with us. She would be delightful company.

CYNTHIA. See, lady, they're all alike.

EDITH. Miss, my dog needs walking. Would you be so kind.

CYNTHIA. I don't see why I shou—

EDITH (*giving* CYNTHIA *the leash*). Here, take his leash

and come back later. (*Shoving* CYNTHIA *out D.L.*) Take him on a long walk.

CYNTHIA. Well, you don't have to shove.

EDITH. Go along with you.

CYNTHIA. All right, but I'll be back, and take my place on the bench. I've got just as much right as the rest of you.

(CYNTHIA *exits with* TOTO's *leash D.L.*)

EDITH (*crossing to L. end of bench*). Andrew, you should be ashamed. A man your age staring at lewd women.

ANDREW (*sitting R. end of bench*). I don't see anything wrong—

EDITH (*crossing behind bench to* ANDREW's *R.*). Did you know her in Germany?

ANDREW. In Germany? I don't think so.

EDITH. She said she knew an Andrew in Germany during the war.

ANDREW. There are hundreds—

EDITH. I know. Did you know her?

ANDREW (*rising*). Now, love, you've been with me every time I went to Germany.

(EDITH *starts crying.*)

Now what's the matter?

EDITH. I've never been to Germany. I've given you the best years of my life, and you have been unfaithful to me. And not only were you unfaithful, but you want her to go on the bus with us on our last trip together.

ANDREW. Now, now, Edith.

EDITH. And we had planned on it for so long.

ANDREW. There's not any good reason to get upset.

EDITH. And after this you were going to write your memoirs.

ANDREW. Now, Edith—

EDITH. And I was going to be your faithful secretary— just like I have always been your faithful secretary.

ANDREW. If you don't want her, she shan't go.

EDITH. And you'll promise never to think of her again.

ANDREW. I promise.

EDITH. I knew you wouldn't let her beguile you. I had faith in you, Andrew, only I—

ANDREW. What is it, my pet?

EDITH. I became suspicious because I was so jealous— you will forgive me for that, won't you?

ANDREW. Certainly, my dear.

EDITH. Because we must stick together, Andrew.

ANDREW. Yes, we must.

(ANDREW *takes* EDITH's *hands, sits her beside him on the bench*, ANDREW *L.*, EDITH *R.*)

EDITH. Because we haven't got anybody else but each other.

ANDREW. Only each other.

EDITH. And Toto and Feathers.

ANDREW. And Toto and Feathers. But, look, Edith, would it really matter if I told her she could go on the bus with us?

EDITH. Andrew, you mustn't let yourself think like that.

ANDREW. Of course not.

EDITH (ANDREW *glows with each adjective*). Because that woman is a wicked, evil, sinful, lustful Jezebel!

ANDREW. Yes!

EDITH. Andrew!

ANDREW. I've changed my mind. If you aren't willing to let her on the bus, I shall not be willing to take my last trip.

(CYNTHIA *enters with the leash, D.L.*)

EDITH. That wasn't a very long walk.

CYNTHIA (*crossing with leash to D.L. end of bench*). Your dog wasn't very anxious to exercise.

ANDREW (*rising*). Oh, miss, I have decided to tell you that you can go with us on the trip.

CYNTHIA. What does your wife say?

ANDREW. It doesn't matter what she says.

EDITH (*rising*). Oh, yes, it does. Our marriage is fifty-fifty. Miss, you cannot go.

CYNTHIA. If your husband says I can, I'm going just to prove to you that he isn't as faithful as you say he is.

EDITH (*stepping down to* CYNTHIA). We've never had

any use for women like you. I don't know why you continue to hang around.

CYNTHIA. The supply is to meet the demand.

EDITH. There would be no demand, if you would get married and behave yourselves like sensible women.

CYNTHIA. If the world depended on sensible women, what use would it have for nonsense like you!

EDITH. The supply is to meet the demand!

ANDREW (*trying to step between* EDITH *and* CYNTHIA). Ladies—

CYNTHIA (*rebuffing* ANDREW). Don't go barking my words back at me.

EDITH. You taught them to me.

CYNTHIA. I taught you everything you know, and look what good it's done you.

ANDREW. Ladies—

EDITH. Past desire? Past hope?

ANDREW. Edith!

CYNTHIA. So you might as well throw in the rouge and lipstick. I'm taking over now.

EDITH. Oh, no, you're not! Andrew and I haven't come this far together to be separated by something like you!

CYNTHIA. Separation began years ago—in Germany!

EDITH (*as she begins to attack* CYNTHIA *physically*). We'll see whose Germany came between us.

CYNTHIA (*fighting*). Oh, yeah!

EDITH. Yeah!

ANDREW. Edith! Cynthia!

EDITH. Leave us alone, Andrew. We've got to settle this ourselves.

CYNTHIA (*to* ANDREW). Yeah, you were the cause of it all, but we've got to settle this ourselves.

ANDREW. Ladies, please! (*He tries to separate the women.*) Please! Please! (*He stands between them, propping them apart.*) I can't keep it up any longer. I'm old, I'm tired—past desire—past hope.

EDITH. You must never say past hope, Andrew.

ANDREW. I can't let you women fight like this.

EDITH. Andrew, this has got to be settled.

ANDREW. But it doesn't make any sense. Don't you remember, Edith, you started this all over a bus trip.

EDITH. You started it! Over *our* bus trip! Our *last* bus trip!

ANDREW. But it's senseless, Edith. There is no bus.

EDITH. No bus?

ANDREW. No bus!

EDITH. You jest.

ANDREW. No, Edith, there is no bus. It was all a game. You know it, and I know it. We just have our little game every Saturday morning to pass the time. But I can't let you take it this seriously. There is no bus station. This is the city park. There is no ticket seller—his office window is the mail box. There is no bus, and we're not going anywhere.

EDITH. Why, Andrew, how dare you say such a thing.

ANDREW. And what's more, we've never gone anywhere, and never will go anywhere—I just keep up the game because you love to sit and wait for the bus. A fight between you women is useless.

EDITH. I am surprised at you, Andrew, I really am surprised. After this trip you were going to write your memoirs.

ANDREW. I decided while in the comfort station that it is useless. There is nothing to write.

EDITH. But your notebooks.

ANDREW. There aren't any notebooks.

EDITH. And your battles in memory.

ANDREW. I was never anything but a private for two years.

EDITH. No, Andrew, you fought in the Battle of Old Baldy, in the invasion of Iwo Jima, the Battle of Argonne Forest; you led the troops at Waterloo and Saratoga. You defeated the Spanish Armada; you helped Saint Joan at Orleans; you fought in the Battle of Hastings, the Battle of Tours, the Battle of Metaurus, the Battle of Marathon, and the Battle of Jericho.

ANDREW. Not I.

EDITH. Yes, you, Andrew. And think of all the things

you invented—the wheel, the lever, the telescope, the printing press with moveable type, the slide rule, the steam engine, the jet plane, the lawn mower, the hydrogen bomb, television, the space satellite, the mousetrap, the electric train, the electronic brain, penicillin, the underwater fountain pen, the zipper, and the hairpin that holds everything together.

ANDREW. Fancy—deception—illusion—dust.

EDITH. You must write your memoirs for those who come after.

ANDREW. There'll be no one to read them.

EDITH. You're wrong, Andrew. There's the orangoutang, the gibbon, the passenger pigeon, the panda, the polar bear, the possum, the whale, the dodo, the angleworm, the salmon, the brontosaurus, the ostrich, the auk, the lyrebird, the tortoise, the buzzard, the hydra, the beetle, the scorpion, and the ant—remember the ant, Andrew, how wise, how frugal, how industrious—you always did underestimate the ant.

ANDREW. You can see, she's quite mad.

EDITH. Then there are the children. We mustn't give up for their sake—the white ones, the pink ones, the yellow ones, the red ones, the brown ones, the mulatto ones, the burnt sienna ones, the black ones, the grey ones, and the olive ones.

ANDREW. We haven't any children really.

EDITH. You mustn't give up now, Andrew. Just when things are looking up. Toto did his trick when you left. Come show him, Toto.

ANDREW. Toto isn't there either.

CYNTHIA. I know. Pitiful, isn't it.

EDITH. And Feathers spoke while you were gone, not in just one language, but many—in English, French, German, Latin, Lithuanian, Czechoslovakian, Russian, Chinese, Korean, Japanese, Arabic, Hebrew, Greek, Egyptian, Sanscrit, Hieroglyphics, Braille, lip reading, Morse code, Semaphore, and one hundred and eighty-seven Indian dialects, and you know what she said in every language—"God is love." That's what Feathers said—"God is love," in every language in the world. And that's why you can't give up, Andrew. You must write your memoirs. This may only seem a game to you, but it's a *real* game!

ANDREW. She's quite harmless. I think she's had too much sun today.

EDITH. Andrew, it's time for the bus. We mustn't miss it. Will you step to the curb and see if it's coming?

CYNTHIA. I guess you should humor her.

ANDREW. That's the best way. (*To* EDITH.) Of course, my dear.

(ANDREW *starts out D.R.*)

EDITH. But be careful.

ANDREW. Certainly, I am always careful.

(ANDREW *exits D.R.*)

EDITH. I guess that shows you whom he listens to.

CYNTHIA. I don't want him.

(*There is the sound of screeching brakes, and the thud of a vehicle against a soft, heavy object. Crowd noises increase.*)

EDITH. What was that?

CYNTHIA. I'll go see.

(CYNTHIA *exits D.R.*)

EDITH (*crossing to bench*). Toto, let me straighten your bow for the trip. There, Feathers, settle down for the bus ride.

(CYNTHIA *returns D.R.*)

CYNTHIA. Lady, your husband—

EDITH. Andrew?

CYNTHIA. He's dead. The bus killed him.

(EDITH *is stunned a moment, then sits on the bench.*)

EDITH (*hesitant, tearfully*). I told Andrew something would happen if he didn't get his glasses changed. Who will ever take his place?

(EDITH *is answered only by the sounds of the animals in the zoo,* TOTO, *the dog, and* FEATHERS, *the para-keet, who seem to be saying "God is Love," in all the languages of the world.*)

CURTAIN